3D Printing with SketchUp

Real-world case studies to help you design models
in SketchUp for 3D printing on anything ranging from
the smallest desktop machines to the largest industrial
3D printers

Marcus Ritland

[PACKT] open source*
PUBLISHING   community experience distilled

BIRMINGHAM - MUMBAI

3D Printing with SketchUp

First published: May 2014

Production Reference: 1140514

Published by Packt Publishing Ltd.
Livery Place
35 Livery Street
Birmingham B3 2PB, UK.

ISBN 978-1-78328-457-3

www.packtpub.com

Cover Image by Marcus Ritland (marcus@denali3ddesign.com)

Credits

Author
Marcus Ritland

Reviewers
Bradley Rubin
Chris Thompson
Samson Tiew

Commissioning Editor
Julian Urssel

Acquisition Editor
Nikhil Chinnari

Content Development Editor
Govindan K

Technical Editors
Arwa Manasawala
Anand Singh

Copy Editors
Mradula Hegde
Laxmi Subramanian

Project Coordinators
Sanket Deshmukh
Sageer Parkar

Proofreaders
Simran Bhogal
Stephen Copestake
Maria Gould

Indexers
Hemangini Bari
Tejal Soni
Priya Subramani

Production Coordinator
Adonia Jones

Cover Work
Adonia Jones
Komal Ramchandani

About the Author

Marcus Ritland is a designer and 3D printing consultant at his small business, Denali 3D Design. Since 2008, he has used SketchUp for architectural rendering services, learning it and helping others well enough to be chosen as "Top SketchUcator" of the SketchUcation forums. After learning about 3D printing through an online contest, he incorporated it into his business, selling 3D-printed goods online and helping other small business owners leverage the technology.

He has also volunteered at a local makerspace, teaching SketchUp classes and leading 3D-printing meetups. He is currently on a quest to eliminate design-for-3D-printing illiteracy. When he's not push-pulling a model into shape, he can be found shooting photos and enjoying nature.

About the Reviewers

Bradley Rubin began using 3D printing while getting his Bachelor of Architecture degree from the Syracuse University. With a passion for storytelling and design, he has worked in both the digital and physical world of film entertainment. Brad's credits include working on films such as This is 40, The Internship, The Muppets, Real Steel, and The Hunger Games. He has worked on multiple films in the capacities of graphic consultant and as an illustrator/3D modeler. Brad spent three years in Boston working as an architect, and did volunteer work that promoted design and architecture to children and Boston area citizens.

Chris Thompson began his career in 3D printing at Hive76 hackerpsace, where he printed his first ever object: a dovetail joint, modeled in SketchUp and printed on a Cupcake CNC. He furthered his skills by building a RepRap and running 3D printer building workshops for new users.

Prior to this, he was a Technical Supervisor at NextFab Studio in Philadelphia and an expert in the field of digital manufacturing. He is also a mildly successful entrepreneur with `meatcards.com`. His previous positions gave him experience with laser engravers, fine hand skills, and digital design tools.

I'd like to thank Valeria, without whom nothing is possible.

Samson Tiew is a co-founder of The make lab, an online digital fabrication platform servicing the Australian market. Coming from an architecture background, he identified a gap in the market to make digital fabrication more accessible to retail customers. Within the field of design and fabrication, he is highly interested in the idea of experimental practices fused with practical experiments.

The make lab is a platform for designers and enthusiasts to fabricate and manufacture customized products. Albeit focusing on laser cutting in the interim, the personnel that form The make lab are very much in tune with other digital fabrication techniques such as CNC routing and 3D printing.

www.PacktPub.com

Support files, eBooks, discount offers and more

You might want to visit www.PacktPub.com for support files and downloads related to your book.

Did you know that Packt offers eBook versions of every book published, with PDF and ePub files available? You can upgrade to the eBook version at www.PacktPub.com and as a print book customer, you are entitled to a discount on the eBook copy. Get in touch with us at service@packtpub.com for more details.

At www.PacktPub.com, you can also read a collection of free technical articles, sign up for a range of free newsletters and receive exclusive discounts and offers on Packt books and eBooks.

http://PacktLib.PacktPub.com

Do you need instant solutions to your IT questions? PacktLib is Packt's online digital book library. Here, you can access, read and search across Packt's entire library of books.

Why Subscribe?

- Fully searchable across every book published by Packt
- Copy and paste, print and bookmark content
- On demand and accessible via web browser

Free Access for Packt account holders

If you have an account with Packt at www.PacktPub.com, you can use this to access PacktLib today and view nine entirely free books. Simply use your login credentials for immediate access.

Table of Contents

Preface

My journey into the fascinating world of 3D printing began in 2010 when I entered a 3D-printing design contest. While I didn't win the contest, I discovered a world of democratized manufacturing, where anyone could create nearly any design with a technology that was once available only to large corporations.

The new idea that 3D printers could create end-use products instead of just prototypes spawned several print-on-demand businesses that drove demand for 3D printed products and drastically reduced prices. Another important factor in the spread of 3D-printing was the expiration of patents that allowed for the development of cheap 3D printers.

Along my journey, I discovered that 3D modeling skills are difficult for many people to master, but masters of the craft are well rewarded. I also found it nearly impossible to get technical help in making printable SketchUp models, and ended up figuring out problems on my own. As I learned, I helped others in online communities use SketchUp to design their models for printing, and as a result my skills improved further.

In these early years of 3D printing for the masses, I see a real need for quality training that allows anybody to use the printers to their full potential. 3D modeling skills are not common even among the early 3D printer adopters, who are often stuck with printing what others make available online.

I sincerely hope this guide saves you from the many difficulties I had when learning to design models for printing.

The 3D printed lamp in the cover image was the author's first design made specifically for 3D printing. Printed in laser-sintered nylon, the lamp throws a unique pattern of light. It was designed entirely in SketchUp, and the complex geometry is an excellent example of what 3D printing can accomplish.

What this book covers

Chapter 1, Concepts Every 3D Printing Designer Needs to Know, introduces different 3D printing processes, each with its pros and cons. You will learn how to find material specifications and choose based on your needs.

Chapter 2, Setting Up SketchUp for 3D Printing, explains how to install SketchUp and customize a template that will allow you to model for 3D printing efficiently. Extensions are introduced, and you make your first 3D printable file.

Chapter 3, From 2D Drawing to 3D Model, shows how to import an image to begin modeling from and how to accurately scale your model. You also learn about importing vector artwork to start your 3D model.

Chapter 4, Understanding Model Resolution, explains segmented curves in SketchUp and how to make your curved models print smoothly. You learn about wall thickness and how to minimize print material. Finally, you learn how to use the Outer Shell tool to combine simple parts into a complex model.

Chapter 5, Using Existing Models, introduces online 3D model repositories, and explains how to make the most of them to save you time. You will learn how to adapt existing models to your needs.

Chapter 6, Designing a Phone Cradle, introduces some advanced modeling techniques and explains how to save time by drawing only half of your model. You see how iterating a model works to gradually improve the final design.

Chapter 7, Importing Terrain and Printing in Color, shows how to import 3D terrain from Google Earth and make it solid for printing. You learn about solid colors and textures in SketchUp and how that affects packaging the model for the printer.

Chapter 8, Modeling Architecture for 3D Printing, shows how to use existing architectural models as a template for making a 3D printable model. You also learn how to split a model into parts to minimize support structures on a desktop FFF printer.

Appendix, Resources for Your 3D Printing Success, provides troubleshooting help and links to other resources to help you make 3D-printable models.

What you need for this book

We need either SketchUp Make or SketchUp Pro. Pro is necessary for commercial users, as per the licensing agreement.

You also need at least a basic knowledge of the SketchUp tools. If you are new to SketchUp, I recommend the book *SketchUp for Dummies, Aidan Chopra, John Wiley & Sons*, or the video training series at `www.go-2-school.com`.

Who this book is for

This book is for SketchUp users who need to physically hold their models, hobbyists and inventors looking to test their prototypes, and students looking to learn about 3D printing.

Conventions

In this book, you will find a number of styles of text that distinguish between different kinds of information. Here are some examples of these styles, and an explanation of their meaning.

Code words in text, database table names, folder names, filenames, file extensions, pathnames, dummy URLs, user input, and Twitter handles are shown as follows: "The 3D model is exported to a format that a slicing program can read, usually Stereolithography [`.STL`]."

New terms and **important words** are shown in bold. Words that you see on the screen, in menus or dialog boxes for example, appear in the text like this: "You can also smooth the imported models easily by selecting their groups and adjusting the slider in the **Soften Edges** dialog box."

 Warnings or important notes appear in a box like this.

 Tips and tricks appear like this.

Reader feedback

Feedback from our readers is always welcome. Let us know what you think about this book—what you liked or may have disliked. Reader feedback is important for us to develop titles that you really get the most out of.

To send us general feedback, simply send an e-mail to feedback@packtpub.com, and mention the book title via the subject of your message.

If there is a topic that you have expertise in and you are interested in either writing or contributing to a book, see our author guide on www.packtpub.com/authors.

Customer support

Now that you are the proud owner of a Packt book, we have a number of things to help you to get the most from your purchase.

Downloading the color images of this book

We also provide you with a PDF file that has color images of the screenshots/diagrams used in this book. The color images will help you better understand the changes in the output. You can download this file from https://www.packtpub.com/sites/default/files/downloads/4573OS_Images.pdf.

Errata

Although we have taken every care to ensure the accuracy of our content, mistakes do happen. If you find a mistake in one of our books—maybe a mistake in the text or the code—we would be grateful if you would report this to us. By doing so, you can save other readers from frustration and help us improve subsequent versions of this book. If you find any errata, please report them by visiting http://www.packtpub.com/submit-errata, selecting your book, clicking on the **errata submission form** link, and entering the details of your errata. Once your errata are verified, your submission will be accepted and the errata will be uploaded on our website, or added to any list of existing errata, under the Errata section of that title. Any existing errata can be viewed by selecting your title from http://www.packtpub.com/support.

Piracy

Piracy of copyright material on the Internet is an ongoing problem across all media. At Packt, we take the protection of our copyright and licenses very seriously. If you come across any illegal copies of our works, in any form, on the Internet, please provide us with the location address or website name immediately so that we can pursue a remedy.

Please contact us at copyright@packtpub.com with a link to the suspected pirated material.

We appreciate your help in protecting our authors, and our ability to bring you valuable content.

Questions

You can contact us at questions@packtpub.com if you are having a problem with any aspect of the book, and we will do our best to address it.

1
Concepts Every 3D Printing Designer Needs to Know

The 3D printer is a favorite tool among product designers. With a 3D printer often placed in the same room as the designer, rapid feedback and faster design cycles make it a staple in large companies. But corporations are not the only ones making use of this increasingly popular technology. Individuals are also increasingly using 3D printing for work and play.

Where does the attraction to 3D printing come from? Speed and automation of manufacturing, accessibility to the masses, and increased complexity of designs are some of the reasons.

The hardest part of the 3D printing process is making a 3D printable model. 3D printers automate the build process once a 3D model is complete. It's easy to buy a printer, but it's much more difficult to make or find good quality models.

Why should you learn how to design for 3D printing? Good designers charge $50 per hour and up, with complex designs taking dozens or hundreds of hours, so learning how to model can save you lots of cash if you're developing a model to print. Alternatively, 3D modeling is a skill you can contract out to produce models for others.

When designing for 3D printing, it is essential that you understand how the process works so that your designs actually work in the printer. Although 3D printers can make very complex models, those models must meet a specific criteria to be printable.

In this chapter, we'll discover what 3D printing is, how it works, who uses the technology, when it makes sense to use 3D printing, and why SketchUp is a good tool for the job.

A short background of 3D printing

What is 3D printing? 3D printing is a common term for a manufacturing process where parts are made by adding layers of material one upon other to form the final product. The process was developed in the 1980s, and is commonly known in the commercial industry as *additive manufacturing* or *rapid prototyping*. **Prototyping** is the process of creating a product by improving on a series of designs. Each change in the design is called an **iteration**.

Commercial 3D printers come with hefty price tags ranging from $20,000 to over $1 million. With the recent expiration of some 3D printing patents, hobbyists have developed small, open source 3D printers. These machines, called desktop 3D printers, are cheap enough to allow individuals to own and operate them, which has led to an explosion in both sales of the machines and interest in 3D printing in general.

The 3D printing process

A basic overview of the 3D printing process is as follows:

1. A 3D model is created with a computer program such as SketchUp.
2. The 3D model is exported to a format that a slicing program can read, usually Stereolithography (.STL).
3. The STL file is loaded into the slicing program that creates instructions (g-code) so that the printer knows how to make the model.
4. The printer builds the model, layer upon layer.
5. There may or may not be post processing necessary to finish the model.

3D printing can be compared to 2D printing in some ways. In both types of printing, a printhead moves back and forth across a printbed, depositing material. The difference in 3D printing is that the material has thickness and is repeated layer upon layer. Another similarity is print resolution. In 2D printing, this is described as **dots per inch (DPI)**, whereas in 3D printing this is typically measured in fractions of millimeters or microns. Often 3D printers have settings to print higher or lower resolutions.

There are many different 3D printing processes, including plastic filament extrusion or **fused filament fabrication, (FFF)**, hardening liquid resin polymers, powder-based systems, and lost wax casting from 3D printed wax models. While there are more technologies, these are the most common at this point.

Watching videos of different 3D printing processes is one of the best ways to understand how the process is unique for each material. I've curated a few of the most popular kinds of processes at `http://www.denali3ddesign.com/video` `-guide-to-3d-printing-technologies/`.

Printing support material

An important function of 3D printing is support material that allows for the printing of overhangs. Commercial printers have a system built into the machine for support material. Support material can be uncured powder in the case of power-based machines, or a separate soluble material printed simultaneously in the case of FFF and other machines. Desktop printers are usually limited to printing supports out of the same material as the rest of the print, or applying workarounds that eliminate the need for support material.

In the following figure, you can clearly see the need for support material in the overhanging layers, where the material would otherwise be hanging over open space:

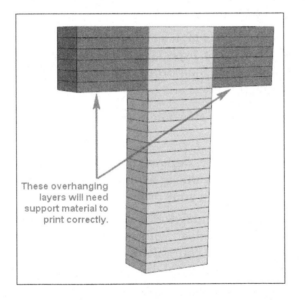

These overhanging layers will need support material to print correctly.

During the design phase, you should think about support material — whether it is necessary and how it can be removed. For example, printing a hollow box with a powder printer will mean designing escape holes for the uncured support powder inside; however, with FFF, escape holes aren't necessary. Often a small tweak in the design phase will make for a much better final print.

Own a printer or use a print service?

While it really depends on the situation, I'm in favor of using a print service for most folks, especially beginners. The following are the reasons:

- Quality is the biggest reason. Print services generally use commercial printers with finishes much better than the typical desktop printer. These services also offer post processing such as polishing or dying the parts with commercial grade equipment.

- Owning a printer also means an upfront investment in equipment and supplies. Much like computers, the technology is improving quickly, so in a few years your system may be outdated and you'll want to purchase a new one. With a print service, somebody else is investing their money, so you just have to pay for the finished parts.

- Print services offer a range of materials and finishes for each material, ranging from metal to plastic and ceramics. Each of these materials has its own set of equipment to maintain and supplies to have on hand, which is too costly for an individual.

- Consumer printers have a high learning curve compared to commercial printers. Desktop printers, especially those built from kits, are notoriously hard to maintain. To get good prints, printers need to be calibrated correctly, a time-consuming process.

On the other hand, the following are some very appealing reasons to own and operate a desktop printer:

- Although not for everyone, building a printer from a kit of parts holds outstanding educational value in learning how electromechanical systems work and how to maintain your printer.

- There are two major advantages to owning a printer, time being the big one. If you're developing a product, your cycle will move fastest if you have a printer in your office. You can walk over in a few hours and pick up your print rather than waiting several days or weeks to receive a part in the mail.

- If you have enough print volume, the overall part cost is also going to be as much as 95 percent cheaper on your desktop printer. Commercial machines are expensive to operate, and when you buy parts from a print service, you're paying for the cost of the printer as well as human labor to make that part.

Perhaps the best option, if your budget allows, is to prototype parts on your own desktop printer, and then use a print service for final, high quality parts. In this way you get the best of both worlds.

Making the most of 3D printing

In what situations does it make sense to use 3D printing technology? Here are a few examples of how people are successfully using 3D printing:

- Inventors use 3D printers to rapidly create prototypes for testing. When you can print an idea and test it a few hours later, your design cycle improves, which helps to get the product to market faster.

- Inventors may also sell 3D prints as finished products before mass-producing. The Glif is a great case study of a design team that 3D printed their first batch of iPhone-to-tripod adapters. (`http://www.therussiansusedapencil.com/post/2794775825/idea-to-market-in-5-months-making-the-glif`).

- Designers can use a 3D print service to make and sell their designs online. This works well because you can focus on making more designs, and let somebody else take care of producing and distributing the finished products. Bathsheba Grossman is a great case study of an artist using a print service for manufacturing and selling her designs online (`http://www.bathsheba.com/`).

- Hard-to-find replacement parts can be made with 3D printing. Some examples are old architectural hardware, antique car parts, and obsolete equipment. This case study explains how a landlord saved hundreds of dollars by printing window parts that are not manufactured any longer (`http://www.denali3ddesign.com/landlord-3d-printing-replacement-window-parts/`).

Designing for prototypes versus finished products

When modeling for 3D printing, there are two ways to approach the design—either you'll be prototyping before traditional manufacturing or designing products specifically for 3D printing and ready-to-use right out of the printer.

If you design for prototyping before traditional manufacturing such as injection molding, then you'll want to design as per the injection modeling guidelines and find a 3D printing technology to fit the specifications of your model. Do not change the design to accommodate a specific 3D printing process, but rather look for a 3D printing process that will meet your prototyping needs.

If you are designing specifically for 3D printing, then you must understand and design around the specific requirements for the material of your choice. For example, in SLS printing, no details smaller than 0.2 mm will show on your model, but for 3D printed ceramic, details must be larger than 2 mm. This is important to know, because if you're printing the same model in different materials, you may need to tweak the design for each material.

If using a 3D print service, look for guidelines on their website that describe how to design for each material. Alternatively, if operating a printer yourself, find the manufacturer's guidelines for model specifications.

Avoiding the pitfalls of 3D printing

I have already mentioned some advantages of 3D printing in one of the previous sections. While 3D printers can make very complex objects with ease, they're not the best solution in other cases for the following few reasons:

- No efficiency gain when making multiple prints of the same model
- It's expensive for parts larger than your hand, particularly on industrial printers
- There is often a lot of hands-on processing of the design, both in the CAD design as well as finishing off the part
- The range of materials is very limited compared to standard manufacturing

Let's discuss these points in more detail. 3D printing is expensive compared to mass manufactured parts (but not compared to one-off or hand-made parts). This is because each part takes just as long to make as the last—there is no time gained by making 50 parts versus just one part.

When doubling the size of a 3D print, you're actually increasing the time to print as well as the volume of the material by eight times. This increases the cost exponentially. For this reason, you'll often see light, airy, almost skeletal designs for 3D printing, as these decrease the volume of material needed. Creating holes in your design makes the part cheaper to print.

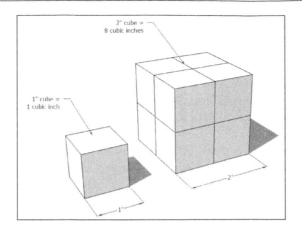

You can also print lower resolutions for thicker layer heights and a faster print, or higher resolutions for thinner, more detailed layers. Making each layer thinner increases the overall number of layers printed. Similar to increasing the size of a print, print time increases when printing a model at higher resolutions.

Visible layer lines are a fact of life with 3D prints. However, it is possible to get a smooth finish on your 3D printed part with some post processing work. Depending on the material, it may be tumbled, sanded, painted, or otherwise worked. This is typically done by hand—a time-consuming process.

Currently, nearly all printers just use one material. This means that if you need multiple materials in one print, you'll have to print them separately and assemble them later. Many materials are not compatible with 3D printing processes, limiting your choices even further.

Choosing a 3D modeling program

There are dozens of 3D modeling programs available, some are free while others cost thousands of dollars. Why use SketchUp?

SketchUp Make is free for non-commercial use, is easy to learn, has a great community of users that you can ask for personalized help, and is customizable through its extensions system. Concepts learned in SketchUp are transferrable if you decide to move on to another modeling program.

SketchUp works best on rectilinear and geometric-type models, but not as well on curvy, organic models. For these kinds of designs, there are tools better suited to the task.

This book is meant to instruct you in how to use SketchUp specifically for 3D printing, but will teach little general SketchUp modeling. If you're new to SketchUp, I recommend SketchUp's own video training series that are available at http://www.sketchup.com/learn/videos, or refer to *Google SketchUp 8 for Dummies, Aidan Chopra, December, 2010,* or the website http://www.go-2-school.com/, in addition to using this book for the specifics of 3D printing.

Summary

3D printing is a fantastic new technology that takes many forms. Knowledge of these technologies is imperative to help you choose the right one for your application. Desktop and commercial printers work very differently and each has its own benefits. Use each for its own advantages.

You must understand the limitations of the technology, and play to its strengths. You wouldn't use a 3D printer to mass manufacture full size cars (yet), just as it's not feasible to manufacture customized phone cases with traditional methods.

Learn about the specifications of your chosen printer/material. Design your model around those specs. SketchUp is a good general purpose modeling tool, but it's not the only one. Learn about other modeling programs, and use the one that best fits your needs.

In the next chapter, you'll learn how to set up SketchUp for 3D printing success.

2
Setting Up SketchUp for 3D Printing

In this chapter, we'll install SketchUp and learn the settings that will make modeling for 3D printing faster and easier. We'll learn about SketchUp extensions, which are essential add-ons for the work we'll be doing.

Downloading and installing SketchUp

SketchUp works on both Windows and Mac, and comes in a free version called SketchUp Make, or a commercial-use version called SketchUp Pro. To download, go to www.sketchup.com. You'll be asked how you plan to use the program, either for personal, commercial, or educational use, and then will be directed to a page to download SketchUp. Make, which is excellent for designing 3D-printable models for non-commercial use, comes with an 8-hour trial version of Pro.

This book uses commands and screenshots from SketchUp 2014 for Windows. Commands in earlier or later versions of SketchUp and SketchUp for Mac may vary slightly from those shown in the screenshots and written commands. All of the exercises in this book can be completed with either SketchUp Make or SketchUp Pro.

Once you've installed the program and opened it, you'll see a splash screen where you'll need to choose a default template as shown in the following screenshot. Scroll to the bottom of the list and choose the **3D Printing – Millimeters** template. After the first time, you won't need to choose a template again, but you will see the splash screen every time SketchUp opens unless you purchase a Pro license:

The SketchUp interface

When opening SketchUp for the first time, you'll see a screen similar to the one shown in the following screenshot:

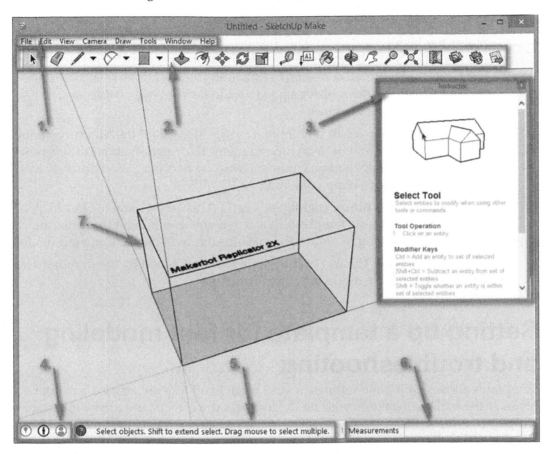

The interface is simple, yet is able to show all the information you need. Let's walk through each of the elements in more detail:

- **Menu bar** highlighted as (**1**): This is your command center, where you can access every tool and command in the program.

- **Toolbar** highlighted as (**2**): This is the **Getting Started** toolbar. There are many more toolbars, and they can be placed around the screen wherever you like.

- **Dialog box** highlighted as (**3**): This is **Instructor**, which shows you what each tool does as you choose it. There are more dialog boxes available in the **Windows** menu.

- **Shortcuts** highlighted as (**4**): This is a mini toolbar to various dialog boxes. You cannot move this toolbar.

- **Status bar** highlighted as (**5**): This area provides you with hints about how to use the active tool with modifier keys. Many tools in SketchUp use modifier keys, such as *Shift*, *Ctrl*, or *Command* (Mac), and *Alt* or *Option* (Mac) to extend the functionality of the tool. It's a good idea to keep an eye on this area, especially if you're a beginner.

- **Value Control Box (VCB)** highlighted as (**6**): Also called the **Measurements** toolbar, this provides you with measurement information about the current operation, and shows certain commands as you're typing. You don't click on it, only watch what's happening in it.

- **3D Printer Build Volume** highlighted as (**7**): This area is new to SketchUp 2014 in the 3D Printing templates. It is a dynamic component that you can adjust to show the build area of the machine that will be printing your model.

- **The drawing area**: The rest of the window is dominated by the drawing area. This is where all the modeling action happens!

Setting up a template for fast modeling and troubleshooting

Templates allow you to save settings in your model and quickly access them later. Styles in SketchUp affect how your model looks on the screen, and are included in templates. With styles, you can add shadows, different color backgrounds, and line weights. While the settings are useful for presenting architectural models, they don't really help while modeling for 3D printing. Even worse, they make SketchUp run slower because the computer has to work harder displaying those extra visuals.

Style settings can be found by navigating to **Window | Styles**. Play around with different styles to see how they change the look of the model. The 3D Printing template that we chose when starting SketchUp has good settings such as a plain background and shadows turned off, but let's tweak it to help with troubleshooting. In the **Styles** dialog box, choose **Default Styles**, then **3D Printing Style**.

Click on the **Edit** tab in the **Styles** dialog box, then click on the **Face Settings** tab, then click on the box beside **Back color** as shown in the following screenshot:

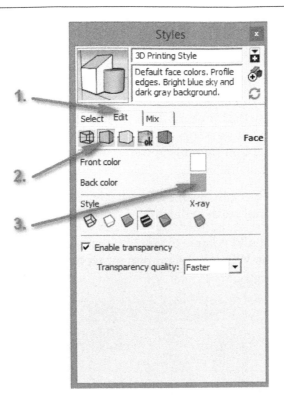

In the window that pops up, choose a nice bright color, say, orange. What this does is make it easy to differentiate front and back faces while modeling. This is important because all faces in SketchUp have a front side and a back side. The faces need to be oriented with the front faces pointing out, and all the back faces pointing inside, or the model will not print correctly.

> Changing the back face to a bright color will allow you to see reversed faces easily, so you can fix them with a simple right-click on the screen and clicking on **Reverse Faces**.

Click on the **Update Style with changes** button at the top right of the **Styles** dialog box, and then close the **Styles** window.

Using the 3D printer's build volume component

The 3D printer build volume model included with the 3D printing templates in SketchUp 2014 gives you a visual representation of the 3D printer's build platform so that you can ensure that your model will fit in the printer properly. The build volume model is a dynamic component—a special model whose measurements you can define via the **Component Options** (or **Component Attributes** if you're using SketchUp Pro) dialog box.

This model will be especially useful if you have a desktop printer. If you're using a print service, you may wish to delete this component.

To set the size of the build volume to your printer, select the build volume component, then go to **Window | Component Options**. You'll see something like the following image.

The drop-down menu lists about 20 of the most popular desktop 3D printers. Choosing a printer from the list and clicking on **Apply** at the bottom automatically resizes the build volume component to the precise size for that printer. My printer, the Solidoodle 2, was not listed. This was not surprising to me, because there are so many desktop printers on the market. In my case, the Printrbot Jr. printer listed is very close in size so I simply used that one.

If your printer is not listed and the available sizes are not close enough, you can easily make a similar component by drawing a box of the size of your printer's build volume, and deleting all faces of the box except the bottom, leaving all edges intact. Make the geometry into a component and delete the original 3D printer build volume component when you're done.

Model units of measurement

You can use SketchUp in either imperial (feet and inches) or metric units. To change the model units, navigate to **Window | Model Info | Units**. You can also switch back and forth between units in the middle of a modeling session with no negative consequences. This is useful when you are modeling in inches, but the 3D printing specs, such as wall thickness, are in metric units. You can design in inches, and then switch to metric units to check measurements and add details.

Many desktop printers are setup to work with mm as default. For this reason, I recommend you use mm for now, and change back to inches later if necessary. Using metric units now will likely save you having to convert units later in your work. If you mostly work with imperial measurements, you may find it easier to go ahead and switch to inches at this point.

Saving our template as the default template

Now that you've gone through all the work of customizing this template, you'll want to save it so you don't have to perform the same steps every time. Before saving, delete all the geometry from the file except the 3D printer build volume component if you want it and perform the following step:

1. Navigate to **Model Info | Statistics**, and click on **Purge Unused**. This clears out any unused styles, components, or other settings that increase the file size.

 To save this template as the default that opens every time you start SketchUp, navigate to **File | Save As Template...** and save it with the name `3D printing mm`. Make sure **Set as Default** is checked before saving. Optionally, fill out the description box with the changes you have made.

Later, as you develop a personalized workflow, you can modify this template to open with nearly any setting or geometry that you wish to begin modeling with. For example, if you model custom Arduino cases, you could start out with a base Arduino model already in your window so that you can start building on top of it right away.

Using other styles

Most of the time, your customized style is the best option, but some of the other styles will be useful as well. The *Architectural Design Style* has thicker lines with tick marks on each line end. This makes the lines easier to see in cases where you may need that option. The other styles are mostly for presentation, and may be useful if you're sharing images of your model with others.

Setting up toolbars

Toolbars allow you to access commands faster than using the drop-down menus in the menu bar. There are many pre-made toolbars, and you can create your own custom toolbars as well.

For starting out, I recommend you turn off the default Getting Started toolbar and place the Standard, Styles, and Views toolbars at the top of your screen, and the Large Tool Set along the left of your screen. The Large Tool Set has many of the tools you'll use while modeling. The Styles toolbar is useful for toggling X-ray mode, and turning colors on and off while modeling. The View toolbar is used for aligning the model to camera views such as Front, Top, or Iso views.

While toolbars are nice for beginners, I recommend you also learn the keyboard shortcuts to speed up your modeling. You can find a one page cheat sheet of keyboard shortcuts at `http://help.sketchup.com/en/article/116693`.

Minimizing dialog boxes

There are a few dialog boxes that you'll use frequently. While you can close them to make more drawing space, and get them back from the **Window** menu when needed, I like to keep the commonly used ones minimized on the right side of my screen. The ones I keep open are as follows:

- Entity Info
- Components
- Materials
- Soften Edges
- Layers

To minimize a dialog box, just click on the top of its window once, and it will roll up so just its name is visible. This way, it stays out of the way but is easily accessible. The boxes stick together, making it easy to keep them looking neat.

The following screenshot is what my screen looks like when I open SketchUp to begin modeling:

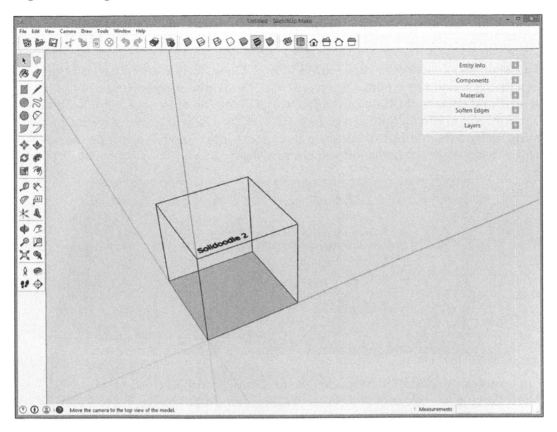

You can see how the drawing space dominates the window. The toolbars are arranged at the top and left side of the window, and the dialog boxes are neatly minimized near the upper right side of the screen.

Installing and using extensions

Extensions, also commonly called **plugins** or **ruby scripts**, transform SketchUp from a cool program for architects into a super versatile modeling tool that nearly anyone can customize to their needs. Extensions in SketchUp 2013 can be installed in a few different ways. The easiest way is via the Extensions Warehouse dialog box inside SketchUp. The first extension we install will allow importing and exporting of files for 3D printing.

Stereolithography [.STL] is the most common file format used as input for 3D printers. SketchUp doesn't natively have the option to export to [.STL], but a couple of generous programmers have written an extension that does just that. They released it for free, as the vast majority of extensions for SketchUp are, and now anybody can generate [.STL] files from their SketchUp models.

To install the extension, navigate to **Window | Extensions Warehouse** and sign in with your Google account. Search for "STL" in the upper-right corner of the screen, and click on the link titled **SketchUp STL** by the SketchUp team. Read the description for info on how to use the extension, and look at the pictures for more info. Click on the red **Install** button in the upper-right corner. A warning message will pop up as shown in the following screenshot:

Click on **Yes**. A confirmation will appear and the extension is ready for use. The following are two more free essential extensions that you'll want to install right away:

- **Solid Inspector** as well as its required component **TT_Lib2**. See extension documentation for the link to TT_Lib2.
- **CleanUp³**.

As with all extensions, read the documentation for instructions on how to use these tools. For example, these three extensions are all accessed in different ways. The STL export/import functions are found under the **File** menu. **Solid Inspector** is found in the **Tools** menu, while Cleanup is in the newly formed **Plugins** menu. Other extensions may be accessed via a toolbar, a menu, or by right-clicking on the screen.

Installing more extensions

The Extensions Warehouse is relatively new, but extensions have been available for several years. How did users install them before the Warehouse? I'm glad you asked, because there are many useful extensions available scattered across the Web that are not in the Extensions Warehouse yet.

To use these other extensions, you must manually place the files into the correct folder on your computer. For more info, visit the help article at `http://help.sketchup.com/en/article/38583`.

The following are the two places to get good SketchUp extensions, besides the Extensions Warehouse:

- **SketchUcation**: This can be found at `http://sketchucation.com/resources/plugin-store-download`. This extension is much like the Extensions Warehouse, but allows installation and management of a huge selection of specialty extensions. SketchUcation is also the best help forum if you get stuck on installing extensions.
- **Smustard**: This can be found at `http://www.smustard.com/`.

You can find more extensions by searching online, but you should install them only if you trust the source.

A quick exercise

Let's make our first 3D-printable model, a simple box with a hole through it. We'll export it as an [.STL], and then import it back to SketchUp to see how the process works by performing the following steps:

1. Draw a 100 x 100 mm square with the **Rectangle** tool.
2. Using **Push/Pull**, pull the square into a 100 mm cube.
3. Draw a circle on top of the square with a 10 mm radius using the **Circle** tool.
4. Push this circle down to the bottom face so it creates a hole through the cube.
5. Select the entire box by triple-clicking on any of its faces.
6. Right-click on **Make Group**. If you look in the **Entity Info** dialog box, it should say **Solid Group (1 in model)**. This is very important! If the model isn't solid, it will not print correctly, so you'll need to go back and fix it.

Use the **Entity Info** dialog box to ensure your model is **solid**.

You should have something like the following diagram with **X-ray** on, so you can see the hole goes all the way through:

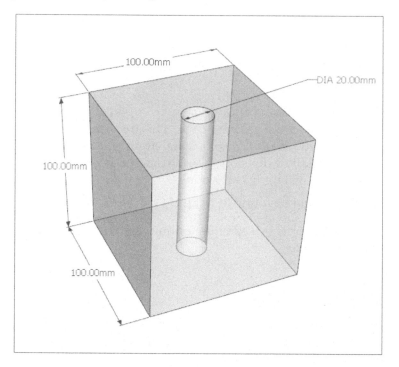

Select the group, and then select **Export STL...** under **File** and save the file with **Units** as **mm**, and **File Format** as **Binary**. Name the file TestCube.stl, making sure to type .stl at the end.

Binary and ASCII STL files are identical for the most part, but binary files are compressed and therefore much smaller and easier to work with.

This file is now 3D printable. You could send this to a printer and have a plastic model in hand within minutes.

Importing .STL files

Select **Import...** under **File**, set the **File type** to [.STL] and navigate to where you saved the [.STL] file. Under **Options**, uncheck **Merge Coplanar Faces**, make sure **Units** are set to **mm**, and then click on **Accept**. Click on **Open** to import the [.STL]. If **Preserve Drawing Origin** is checked in the **Import** options, it will import directly on the first cube you drew, so move it to the side with the **Move** tool.

Now import the same file again, but this time in **Import STL Options**, and check the **Merge Coplanar Faces** box. Once again, move it to the side so you can see all the three boxes — the original SketchUp model and the two imported [.STLs]. You should have something like the following diagram:

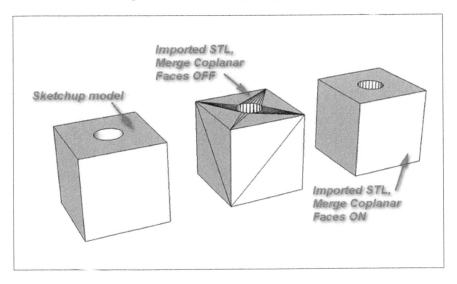

Notice the differences between the three models. The .STL format **triangulates** the model shown by the extra lines you see on the center model. The **Merge Coplanar Faces** command deletes those extra lines upon import so that you can work with imported .STL files more easily. For example, you could easily push/pull the top face of the clean imported model, but for the center model it would be much more difficult because of the extra faces.

Also, notice the difference between the inside of the hole in the SketchUp model versus the imported models. The SketchUp model looks smooth, while the imports are **faceted**, meaning you can see each individual face that makes up the hole. By turning on hidden geometry, **View | Hidden Geometry**; you can see that these are the exact faces in the SketchUp model before exporting.

This is important to know because you can increase the number of sides your circle will have in SketchUp to make the final print smoother and more accurate if necessary. This is discussed further in *Chapter 4, Understanding Model Resolution*. You can also smooth the imported models easily by selecting their groups and adjusting the slider in the **Soften Edges** dialog box.

The CleanUp extension you installed earlier will also merge coplanar faces. This is useful if you're using an older version of SketchUp that doesn't have the option to merge coplanar faces in **STL Import Options**.

Summary

In this chapter, you installed SketchUp and customized a template that will allow you to model for 3D printing quickly. You learned what extensions are, how to install them, and where to find many more that are not available in the official Extensions Warehouse.

You made your first 3D-printable STL file, and imported the file back into SketchUp. Finally, you also learned why it's important to merge coplanar faces on imported STL files. In the next chapter, we'll learn how to design a 3D-printable model starting from a 2D sketch.

3

From 2D Drawing
to 3D Model

One of the simplest kinds of 3D models starts from a simple drawing. Starting with pen and paper, a precise, professionally designed graphic or anything in between, you can quickly make a 3D-printable model. Logos and cookie cutters are some common 3D prints that are made from 2D graphics. In this chapter, we'll create a useful household object, starting from a simple hand-drawn sketch.

Starting from a quick sketch

For this exercise, let's start with something useful, and somewhat simple. But since we're going to 3D print it, we'll make a fun design.

I started by making a pen and paper sketch of my initial concept—a hook-shaped, low-resolution version of a seahorse. I then scanned the image into a JPEG file and saved it to my computer. As you can see in the following figure, it's not a great drawing, but rather a starting point:

Designing for ease of printing

Let's talk about my thought process for this design. I intend for this hook to be printed on a desktop FFF printer. For that reason, I'm going to design parallel lines, no overhangs, and no tiny details. Although more complex designs are certainly printable, this will ensure an easy print from the start. Now, let's model!

Modeling in SketchUp from a sketch

To get started, we need to import the image into SketchUp. Navigate to **File | Import...**; under **Files of type**, click on **All Supported Image Types**; and under **Options**, click on the **Use as image** radio button.

Double-click on the image or select the image and click on **Open** to close the **Import** dialog box, as shown in the following screenshot:

Click near the origin in SketchUp to set one corner of the image, and then move your cursor towards the upper-right side of the screen to set the size of the image. You want the image to be large enough to see but the exact scale isn't important now.

If you draw on the image right now, the SketchUp lines will be hard to see. Let's reduce the opacity of the image to make it easier to draw on. To do so, right-click on the image and click on **Explode**. Right away, double-click on the image to select it and its bounding edges, and then make it into a **Group**.

Open the **Materials** dialog box. Click on the home icon and then click on the **In Model** option. Now, select the imported image. Click on the **Edit** tab and drag the opacity slider down to around 30 percent as shown in the following screenshot:

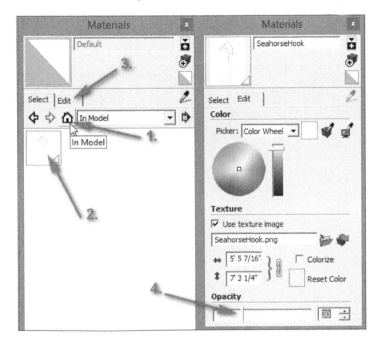

Now we'll scale the image to size. I want the printed hook to be 100 mm tall overall. For this step, the **Tape Measure** tool is fast and accurate. With **Tape Measure**, click on the top point of the seahorse's head, then the bottom flat edge of the hook. Immediately type 100 mm and hit *Enter*. As shown in the following screenshot, SketchUp will ask, **Do you want to resize the model?**; click on **Yes**.

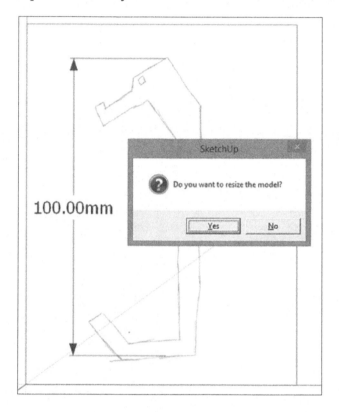

The model will scale to the correct size and may shift out of view. Use the **Zoom Extents** tool to center it back on the screen.

Now we're ready to begin drawing. Using the **Line** tool, trace the sketch, using the sketch as a rough guide, and not as an exact template. Because the sketch lines are probably not perfectly vertical and horizontal, be sure your horizontal and vertical lines in SketchUp align to the red and green axes, and not necessarily align exactly to the sketch.

Start at one point and work your way around the sketch, making sure each line is connected to the last one. Using the left and right arrow keys to lock to the green and red axes may help you at this point.

For the angled lines, I used the **Protractor** tool to create guides at 45 degrees, and traced over the guides. I used the **Tape Measure** tool to create guides for parallel lines. Before you move on to the next step, you should have a continuous outline that creates a face. Draw the eye last, then select and delete the interior face of the eye, as shown in the following figure:

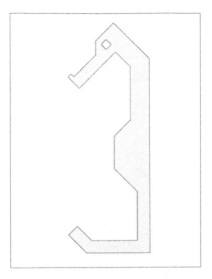

Keeping a historical timeline of changes speeds iteration

Many of the products you use in your daily life are designed in a process where an idea is modeled, manufactured as a prototype, tested, analyzed, and then redesigned to improve functionality. This process of building a design and improving it over time is called **iterative design**, and each new model in the design is one iteration.

When you use a 3D printer to make the prototype, the process goes dramatically quicker, which is where the term **rapid prototyping** comes from. Saving a history of the models made during the design process is a good practice, so you know what changes have been made. One way to keep track of changes is by saving the file with a new version number, such as DesignV1 and DesignV2.

On a model as simple as this seahorse hook, I simply save copies of the new versions inside the original SketchUp model. Taking this idea one step further, I make copies at important stages of the model, even before one design is finished. This way, if you want to make changes to a part of the model when you're nearly finished, you can go back to an earlier stage of the model and work from there, rather than starting completely from scratch.

Let's apply this principle to our model now. Using the **Move** tool + *CTRL*, create a copy of the seahorse outline you just drew a few centimeters away. It's time to go 3D! Use the **Push/Pull** tool and extrude the copied face up. I chose a thickness of 8 mm, as shown in the following figure:

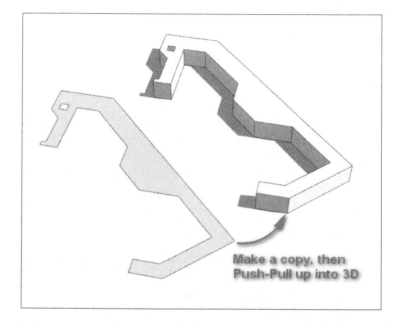

The original outline is still available to copy again, tweak the shape, and change it into an improved design, thereby saving the time it takes to trace the outline again.

Exporting the model and printing

Group the hook, verify that it's solid using the **Entity Info** dialog box, and you're ready to export it as an .STL file for 3D printing after following the steps outlined in *Chapter 2, Setting Up SketchUp for 3D Printing*.

If the group is not solid, look for interior faces, missing faces, or stray lines in the group. Interior faces and stray lines should be deleted, whereas missing faces need to be filled in. The Solid Inspector extension is an excellent tool for finding problems in this step. Refer to the *Appendix, Resources for Your 3D Printing Success* for more detailed information about troubleshooting models.

In the following screenshot, you can see several iterations of hooks that I 3D-printed starting from this exact model:

That completes this exercise. With a little practice, a small project like this will take you less than 15 minutes to go from the sketch to the printer.

Importing vector artwork

Sometimes artwork is available in vector format, having already been drawn in Illustrator or another 2D drawing program. In this case, you can save a lot of tedious tracing work by importing the drawing and using it as a base for your 3D model.

Vector graphics are different from the usual raster images we see that are made of pixels. Unlike raster images that look blurry when zoomed up close, vector graphics can be scaled, re-sized, and zoomed up without any loss of quality. Vector graphics describe the artwork in a way that SketchUp can interpret as lines, saving you from tracing the image manually. As an analogy, you can think of SketchUp models as 3D vector graphics.

In your 2D app, save the artwork as a .DXF file. You may need to add anchor points before exporting so that curves import smoothly. Please see the documentation for your vector graphics app for more info on how to add anchor points. SketchUp Pro natively imports .DWG and .DXF files. SketchUp Make imports .DXF with the Dxf_In plugin (`http://sketchucation.com/forums/viewtopic.php?f=323&t=31186`).

The import process doesn't always work perfectly. There may be tiny gaps between lines, short stray lines, or a variety of other problems. The Edge Tools[2] extension helps with those problems (`https://extensions.sketchup.com/en/content/edge-tools²`).

After importing, create faces inside the drawing outlines by tracing over an edge. For complex models, you may also use the Make Faces plugin to create the faces (`http://www.smustard.com/script/MakeFaces`).

At this point, you can pull the faces into 3D, and manipulate them just as with any other SketchUp geometry.

Changing the scale of the part

For printing in different sizes, you can use either the **Scale** tool or the **Tape Measure** tool just as you learned how to scale the image. The **Scale** tool works best for even increments such as 0.5 size or 3 times larger.

Sometimes you may want to scale along only one axis of a model. This is a job for the **Scale** tool. Learn how the various grips on the **Scale** tool affect the scaling of the model to quickly modify those parts.

The **Tape Measure** tool is a better choice when you know the exact dimensions (for example, 3.5 inches tall) and can measure directly on the part. With **Tape Measure**, pick any two points, and enter the desired dimension. The entire model will change scale uniformly. If you want to change just the scale of one group with **Tape Measure**, then open just that definition for editing and perform the scale operation. Only that group will change size and the rest of the model will remain the same size.

A bonus tip – the 45-degree overhang rule for filament printers

Filament printers perform best when overhangs are supported or are angled at 45 degrees or less. This is because the material must be deposited onto something, usually the layer below. You can see the difference as shown in the following figure:

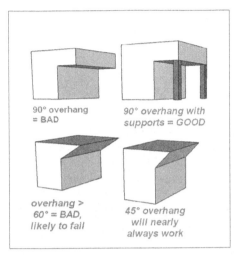

This leads to a common design rule called the "45-degree overhang rule". When designing for filament printers, keep the slope at 45 degrees or less for best results.

Bridging across a short distance (about 2-3 inches should be no problem) as shown in the preceding image, is also a viable solution, but the two sides must be of equal heights. The following figure shows how I added mounting holes for screws in the seahorse hook:

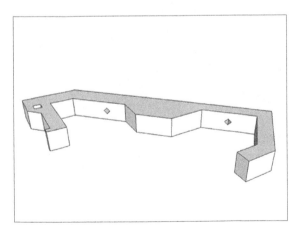

Notice how the holes are in a diamond shape so they meet the 45 degree overhang rule. Holes this small will actually print fine as circles as the filament will bridge the small gap, but for larger holes a diamond shape like this is a good idea.

Making the design your own

To take the design further, you can use the **Arc** tool or Roundcorner plugin to smooth out the sharp corners. You could cut a mounting hole at the back for a magnet, or add seahorse scales for decoration. How would you customize the design to make it your own?

Summary

In this chapter, you learned how to import an image and use the **Tape Measure** tool to scale your model. You learned to make a closed loop of edges to form a face, which may then be pulled up into a 3D shape. The **Tape Measure** and **Protractor** tools are useful for making guidelines to model accurately.

We discussed what iterative design is, and how to efficiently save copies of a model to create a history of changes.

Importing vector artwork created in a 2D drawing app can save you tedious drawing in SketchUp. Export the artwork as .DWG or .DXF to import into SketchUp.

We learned about the 45-degree rule when designing for filament printers. Keeping overhangs to 45 degrees or less results in the best prints. Bridging short distances is also viable when the two sides are of equal height. These principles are discussed further in *Chapter 6, Designing a Phone Cradle*.

4
Understanding Model Resolution

In this chapter, we will learn about wall thickness and some different methods to create the wall thickness you want. We will explore circles, arcs, and how changing the number of segments they are made of affects the appearance of the printed model. We'll learn how to overcome the dreaded *missing faces* problem, which happens frequently when faces are not created at the time of modeling at a small scale in SketchUp.

So, first a bit of high-level theory, and then we'll get to the fun part—modeling the vase in the following figure:

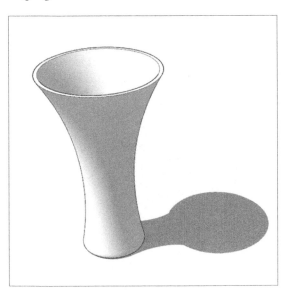

Wall thickness

Wall thickness is a very important concept in 3D printing. Although physics plays no role when designing on your computer, once the design makes it out into the real world, it must abide by the laws of nature.

Because it is so easy to zoom up into any detail of your model and make it fill your screen, a very common problem new designers face is understanding the model's scale in the real world. When holding your very first print, you'll likely be surprised at its size, usually by how small it is. For this reason, even though a design may look just fine on your screen, it can break in real life if its wall thickness isn't strong enough to support it.

At the same time, you don't want your walls to be too thick, or you'll use more material than necessary, costing you more money. Wall thickness is a balance that you as a designer will optimize for each model.

Wire thickness measures the diameter of a cylinder, and typically needs to be slightly larger than the minimum wall thickness. Some examples of wires are tree branches, truss struts, and the arm of a superhero figurine. A tree branch connected at one end would be considered a free wire, while a truss strut connected on both ends is a supported wire.

Detail size is related to wall thickness. For example, if you're printing a scale model of a house, the wall thickness would be the thickness of the structural walls, while the detail size would be how far the window trim sticks out from the wall. In general, detail size is smaller than wall thickness.

Wall thickness and other related requirements depend on the printing process, and vary according to the material choice and printer resolution. If you're using a print service, look for technical specifications on their website. If you own a desktop printer, print resolution will depend on the nozzle size and layer resolution supported by that printer. These specifications will be available on the manufacturers' website.

As an example, the following screenshot shows a partial list of design guidelines for minimum walls, wires, and details in **Strong & Flexible Plastics** available at www.shapeways.com:

Strong & Flexible Plastics

Material Overview	Design Guidelines

Min Wall Supported: 0.7mm

Min Wall Free: 0.7mm

Min Wire Supported: 0.8mm (Unpolished) · 0.9mm (Polished & Dyed)

Min Wire Free: 1.0mm

Min Embossed Detail: 0.2mm (0.5mm is recommended for readable text)

Min Engraved Detail: 0.2mm (0.5mm is recommended for readable text)

Screencap courtesy of www.shapeways.com

As you can see, these are the minimum requirements—you should not design any feature smaller than those indicated, and usually should design most features somewhat larger.

Now let's model!

Modeling a vase

Modeling a vase can be a simple, rewarding exercise to help us understand wall thickness, model resolution (versus layer resolution), and build on our knowledge of overhangs. Adding handles will demonstrate how to use the **Outer Shell** command to combine several solids into a single manifold shell. Follow along in SketchUp as I walk through the steps and thought process I used when creating this vase.

Creating a profile

While there are several ways to model a vase, the easiest is using the **Follow Me** tool. The first step is to create the profile of one half of the vase, as shown in the following figure:

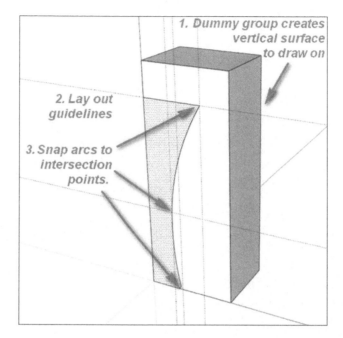

Let's break this figure down. The first thing I did was create a temporary rectangular box larger than the vase profile and make it into a group. I did this so that I had a vertical surface to draw on, making certain the profile is perfectly aligned with the red and blue axes. The box is grouped so the new geometry doesn't stick to it, and I can also use the edges of the box to assist in drawing the vertical and horizontal guidelines in the next step.

The second step was to draw horizontal guidelines (using the **Tape Measure** tool) corresponding to the top edge and the waist of the vase. Then I drew the vertical lines corresponding to the top edge, the base, and the waist. The intersections of these guidelines create points that allow me to accurately place arcs in the next step. The exact size isn't as important at this point as the proportions of the profile but, to give you an idea, the dummy box is 150 mm tall.

Using the **Arc** tool, I connected the intersections for the top, center, and bottom of the vase. Then I used the **Line** tool to draw the top edge, the vertical center line, and the bottom edge of the vase, connecting with the arcs to create the face highlighted in blue in the previous figure.

A face will be created if all connecting edges form an unbroken loop and are on a single plane. This is why the dummy box is so useful—it is much easier to draw on another face than in midair.

Avoiding missing faces by scaling up your model

Often when performing a **Follow Me** operation on a small model, SketchUp fails to form some or all of the tiny faces. The way to prevent this is to scale your model bigger by an easy-to-remember number such as 100, and then perform the operation.

While it is possible to scale the entire model or a portion of the model with the **Scale** tool, I find it easy to forget what scale I'm working at, so I use a simple trick to help me remember. Notice the 50 mm line in the following figure:

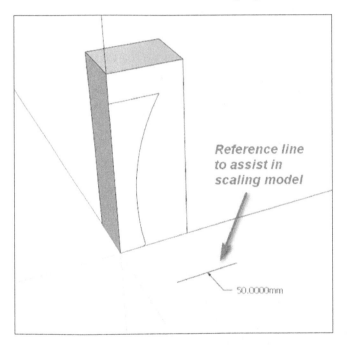

This is a reference line I drew near the origin of the model. Then, I get the **Text** tool by navigating to **Tools | Text** (not the **3D Text** tool) and click on the center of the line. By default the **Text** tool creates a label with the length of the line, helping me remember how long it is supposed to be. The length doesn't matter, just so long as it's an even number and long enough to see easily.

To scale up the model, use the **Tape Measure** tool and click on one end of the line first and then the other. Type in a new measurement, say 5000 mm, and hit *Enter*. SketchUp will ask if you want to resize the model; click on **Yes**.

Now you can perform your operations without any missing faces. When your model is complete, resize the model using the **Tape Measure** tool again, but this time typing in 50 mm, the measurement you created earlier with the **Text** tool.

Creating wall thickness

For our vase example, we'll create a wall thickness of 2 mm. After saving the original vase profile, make two copies of the profile along the red axis. We are making these copies as backups because we can't access the previous state of the model without using the **Undo** command. As we discussed in *Chapter 3, From 2D Drawing to 3D Model*, making a copy in the SketchUp file before you perform important actions creates a historical timeline that you can access in case you want to branch off and try something different.

Select all of the bottom and side arcs; then with the **Offset** tool, offset the lines inward by 2 mm. This creates the wall thickness that we need. Clean up all the extra edges, leaving only the nice, even 2 mm-wide profile shown on the right side of the following figure:

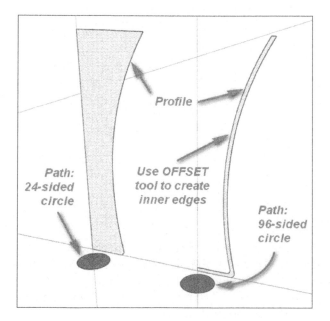

Cleaning up all extra edges is an important step. Zoom up close to see that you erase the tiny ones, too, because even these will cause your model to not become solid.

Notice the vertical guidelines passing through the center line of each profile. Create and use these guidelines to form a circle that you'll use as a path for the **Follow Me** tool in the next step. The guidelines will pass through each circle's center.

Understanding noncircular circles

To help understand the next step, let's take a short break from modeling for some theory. Circles and arcs in SketchUp are made from a number of line segments. You can see this for yourself if you draw a circle and zoom up close to it. By default, there are 24 segments in a circle and 12 segments in an arc. This is important when talking about the resolution of your model.

You can see that, if you draw a circle with radius 50 mm, each of the 24 segments comprising the circle will be about 13 mm long. If you made the circle with a 5 mm radius, the segments would be 1.3 mm long. If you then extrude the two circles into cylinders, the segments form the facets on the cylinder. The 13 mm facets on the large cylinder will be very noticeable, but the 1.3 mm facets on the small cylinder will not show nearly as much, as shown in the following figure:

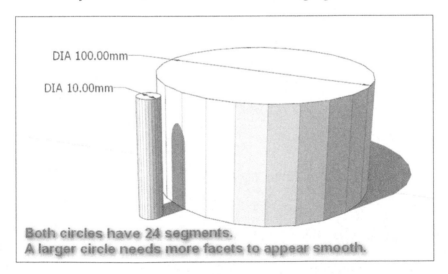

You can easily change the number of segments in circles and arcs in SketchUp before they are extruded (for more details on changing circle segments refer to a help article at http://help.sketchup.com/en/article/94740). Since you cannot change the resolution after extruding, you'll want to think about the resolution at the start.

The length of line segments on your curves forms what I refer to as model resolution. Model resolution affects the appearance of your printed model. If you want a smoother looking model, increase the segment count of curves. In general, if your segments are 1 mm or smaller, you won't notice them on the printed model; however, for high resolution printers, you may want to decrease the resolution to 0.1 mm or even smaller. This is because a higher resolution printer will show facets more clearly and therefore will require a model with more segments in the curves to look smooth.

Making the magic happen with the Follow Me tool

Now for the fun part! Select the circle path first, and then click on the corresponding profile with the **Follow Me** tool. Repeat for the other profile to make two vases as shown in the following figure:

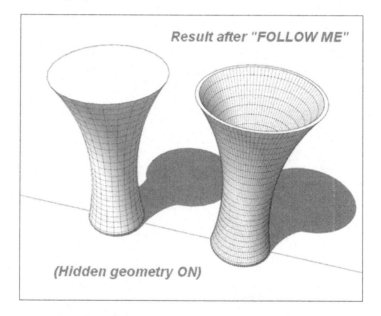

You probably noticed that the circular paths in the figure we saw in the previous section are labeled differently, although from a distance they look the same. The one on the left has 24 segments by default, while I set 96 segments for the one to the right.

Notice how the resulting model on the right has many more segments. With its much higher model resolution, it will look and feel much smoother after 3D printing. Higher segment counts also make more dimensionally accurate curves.

A smart reader will infer that we can also increase the segments of the profile curves in addition to the path curves, and you would be completely correct! You can completely control the resolution of any curves in your model, as long as you adjust them before extruding.

In some cases, you may not want a smoother print for artistic or other reasons. In this case, it is perfectly acceptable to use a lower path resolution.

In the following figure, we can observe that each vase used the exact same profile, but the number of path segments is denoted by the numeral below each vase. Each vase is printable and looks unique from the others:

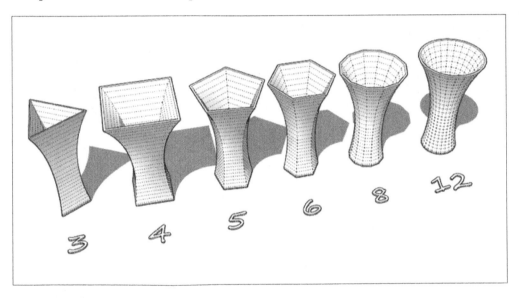

As with wall thickness, the number of segments you use in an arc should be balanced. Too many and you'll increase file size, increase processing time, and have trouble with missing tiny faces; too few and your model will look faceted and unpolished.

A bonus tip for desktop extrusion printers

Notice how I created one vase with 2 mm wall thickness, while the other vase is solid. The solid vase actually prints better on desktop extrusion printers because you can tell the printer to make a certain number of passes around the perimeter, and not fill the center. Keep reading for a photo of the final vase printed using this method!

Combining solids with the Outer Shell tool

When adding major features to your model, I find it useful to keep the parts separate until the end of the modeling process, and then combine them into the final solid printable model. This approach makes it easier to edit the different parts of the model if you ever want to go back and change something.

For example, let's say we want to add handles to our vase. First, make a copy of the vase along the red axis, and make it into a group. Be sure the group is solid before continuing.

In the following figure, I have a dummy group running through the center of the vase. This creates a surface to draw the path for the handle, as shown:

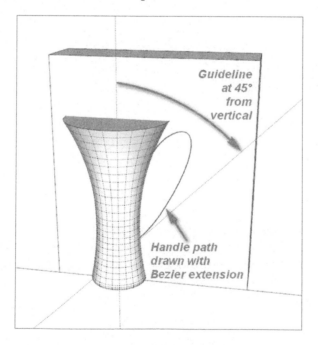

To draw the path for the handle, I used the **BezierSpline** extension by fredo6 http://sketchucation.com/forums/viewtopic.php?t=13563. This extension allows you more freedom than the **Arc** tool when creating curves.

In the previous chapter, we discussed the 45-degree overhang rule for desktop extrusion printers. Since I wanted to print this vase at home, I created a guideline at 45 degrees from the vertical. As long as the handle does not exceed the angle defined by the guide, I know it should print fine.

The next step is to draw the profile for the handle. I used a circle with radius 2 mm and 6 sides (shown at the bottom of the path in the following figure). I deleted the dummy group and used the **Hide** command (right-click on the object and click on **Hide**, or go to **Edit | Hide**) on the vase to temporarily isolate the profile and path:

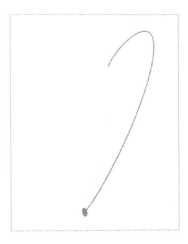

Perform the **Follow Me** operation, and make the resulting handle into a group. Unhide the vase (by going to **Edit | Unhide | Last**). Move the handle slightly so that its ends are completely inside the vase group, as shown in the next figure:

Make a copy of the handle on the opposite side of the vase. Right-click on the handle and go to **Flip Along | Group's Red**, to make a mirror image of the handle. Once again, move it into place so that the ends are completely inside the vase group.

You should now have three solid groups—the vase and two handles. Make a copy of all three along the red axis, helping create that history of important steps in your model. All that remains is to combine them using the **Outer Shell** command into a single solid object, as shown in the following figure. Export it as an .STL file, and you're ready to print!

Ready to print!

The following figure shows the final vase printed on my desktop extrusion printer. The settings I used are 50 percent scale, 0.3 mm layer height, 1 shell (perimeter), 0 percent infill, and no top layer:

The print was a success on the very first try! Designing the handles to meet the 45-degree-overhang rule worked as intended. The printer was able to bridge the short distance connecting the top of the handle when it reached that point. The bridge could have been even smoother if I had slowed down the printer to allow cooling time for the layers below.

Notice the faceting visible on the inside of the vase. By now you know this could have been avoided by increasing the number of segments in the path. On a higher resolution printer the faceting would be even more noticeable; however, on an extrusion printer, the effect is somewhat muted because the bead of plastic slightly bends as it travels around sharp corners.

Bonus – more methods to create wall thickness

Perhaps the easiest way to create an even wall thickness is using the offset method you learned earlier in this chapter. But that method will not work in all cases. In this section, we'll discuss some more methods for creating thickness.

For symmetric shapes, you can copy/paste the shape in place, and use the **Scale** tool to make a smaller version of that part. Scaling from the center or selectively using the various grips, you can manipulate the copied shape to form a wall at a specified distance.

As a simple example, think of a cube—make it a group to keep the geometry from sticking to the copy, copy/paste in place, scale to something less than 100 percent, and you have an interior set of walls. You'll need to explode the groups, reverse the copy's faces, and connect the walls to the original geometry, and you'll have an even wall thickness.

JointPushPull Interactive is a plugin that will also help in creating wall thickness. Authored by fredo6, this plugin is available from SketchUcation at `http://sketchucation.com/forums/viewtopic.php?p=496773`. For more information about how to use this plugin to create thickness on complex geometry, please refer to *Chapter 7, Importing Terrain and Printing in Color*.

Summary

In this chapter, you learned about wall thickness and several methods of creating thickness. Balancing wall thickness to create enough strength without wasting material is a skill you'll learn with practice.

We discussed how adding segments to your curves improves model resolution, and how to balance model resolution with the accuracy of your printer. More curve segments = smoother model = bigger file size. Too large a file size makes SketchUp run slower.

You learned that SketchUp doesn't work well with tiny faces, and an easy trick to scale your model up and back down quickly and accurately. Finally, you saw how keeping major features of your model as separate solids allows for ease of editing until the end of the modeling process. Later, you can use the **Outer Shell** command to combine multiple solids into one for printing.

In the next chapter, we'll learn how to save and reuse models we create. We also discover websites to download 3D models that other designers have made freely available, and how to edit and adapt a model to fit our needs perfectly.

5
Using Existing Models

Copy and paste, one of the best time saving features available in computer programs, works just as you'd expect in SketchUp. You can copy and paste inside a model or between SketchUp models. Using the power of components, you can also easily reuse SketchUp models between modeling sessions.

As you're likely well aware, the Internet has taken copy and paste to the next level with file sharing sites. Much like people use social websites like Instagram to show off their photos, model sharing websites allow 3D modelers to showcase their work. What's more, model sharing sites enable other users to download and remix models, keeping track of the model's popularity with features such as likes and a download counter.

While it's certainly good to have the skills to model anything you want to 3D print, you can often save time by downloading an existing 3D model. Since commonly shared .STL models are meshes much like SketchUp models, SketchUp works well with them and is one of the best ways to edit existing models in the .STL format. You can resize models beyond simple scaling, combine models, or extract a feature for using in another project.

In this chapter, we'll look at best practices of reusing our own models, and how to work with models downloaded from the Internet.

Leveraging SketchUp components to save time

Picture this—Sal has a small business providing customized iPhone cases. He takes orders to print customer's names on a phone case in a color of their choice.

To create a quality case, Sal precisely measured his own iPhone with a pair of calipers, noting overall dimensions and locations of features like the power jack, volume buttons, and the camera. From this data, he modeled a case in SketchUp, printed it, and tested it for fit. The first case was a bit too tight, so he increased the dimensions in SketchUp and tested the print again. After 4 iterations between SketchUp and the printed part, the case snapped crisply onto his phone, all the openings worked well when plugging his phone in and Sal was happy with the case.

Sal's process of printing, testing, and re-designing until getting the exact result he wanted is typical in product design. This is where having a desktop printer shines, since the wait time for prints shrinks to nearly zero. When he needs higher quality prints, he can still order from a print service like Shapeways or i.materialise.

Saving a model as a Component

After modeling the original phone case, Sal saved it as a Component. Components are similar to Groups in SketchUp, but have a few enhanced properties. These are listed as follows:

- The ability to save a component as a separate SketchUp model
- All the copies of a component in a model are changed when one of them is edited
- The ability to use the **Components** window to manage Components
- Create and access local collections (on your computer) of components

In the following screenshot, we'll take a closer look at the **Components** window:

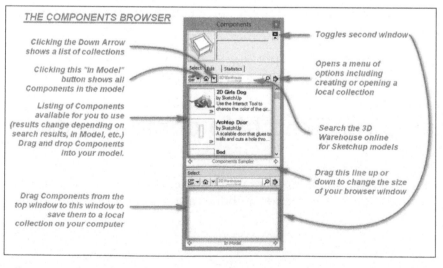

Once you've created a Component in your model, it can be accessed in the **Components** browser. From here, you can drag-and-drop another copy into your drawing window. In the **Components** browser, you can also open a second window under the first, and drag models between the windows to save a component you've created to a local collection on your computer.

To try this yourself, simply perform the following steps with a simple box in place of the phone case:

1. Make the phone case into a Component and save it with the name
   `iPhone 5S Blank Case`.

2. Click on the **In Model** button in the **Components** window to show the phone case component.

3. Toggle the second window so that it is visible.

4. Click on the arrow to the right of the second window, and then open or create a Local Collection. Navigate to a folder.

5. Now, the second window represents the specified folder. Drag the phone case from the top window to the second window. Voilà! The phone is saved to a local collection on your computer.

The next time you need that component, you can open that collection from the **Components** window and drop it directly into a model.

Another way to save components to a local collection is to simply right-click on the component and select **Save as**, and navigate to the folder you want to save it to.

Online 3D model repositories

These websites host collections of 3D models that other users have uploaded. There are dozens of these sites, some with free models and some with models you pay to download. In the following subsections, we will discuss what to expect from the three most popular sites.

Thingiverse

Thingiverse (`http://www.thingiverse.com/`), owned by 3D printer manufacturer Makerbot, is by far the most popular 3D printing model site. Most models are free, but even on free models the uploader may choose to set restrictions on usage, for example, not for commercial use.

Most of the models are in `.stl` format, ready to download and print. Models can be uploaded in nearly any format, including `.skp`.

3D Warehouse

The 3D Warehouse (`http://3dwarehouse.sketchup.com`) is SketchUp's very own repository of models. It's astonishingly extensive—everything from Star Wars X-Wing models and people in various uniforms and poses, to architectural models and useful household objects, and nearly everything in between can be found in the 3D Warehouse.

All models are in `.skp` or another SketchUp compatible format, meaning you can open them in SketchUp without converting the file format. Models can be downloaded using your web browser or directly into your SketchUp model using the Components browser.

Most models in the 3D Warehouse were created for use in visualizations, so they're not built with 3D printing in mind. You will either have to fix them to be printable, or rebuild them to be printable. Rebuilding the model is often the quicker choice. Even if you need to rebuild a model, having a model to start from and use for reference geometry can be a time saver. Rebuilding a model using an existing model as reference is covered in *Chapter 8, Modeling Architecture for 3D Printing*.

GrabCAD

GrabCAD (`https://grabcad.com/`) is popular with professional engineers. Most models are high quality, mechanical type items. Relatively few are in a format compatible with SketchUp, but if you message the model owner and ask nicely, they may convert the model to a format like `.stl` that you can import into SketchUp.

Case study – modifying a GoPro wrench

Kim found a wrench on Thingiverse that she likes for tightening a GoPro camera, but wished the handle was longer. The link to the wrench is `http://www.thingiverse.com/thing:185739`.

Simply scaling the model is easy to achieve with other programs like Netfabb (`www.netfabb.com`) or your desktop printer's slicing program. Scaling would make the handle longer, but would also proportionally increase the size of the wrench head, making it too large for its purpose. Using SketchUp she easily lengthened just the handle.

She downloaded the `.stl` file and opened it in SketchUp. Since she prefers using SketchUp 8, she didn't have the option to merge coplanar faces like we discussed in *Chapter 2, Setting Up SketchUp for 3D Printing*; the model came in triangulated, which is normal for `.stl` files. It looked like the following diagram:

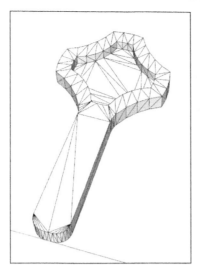

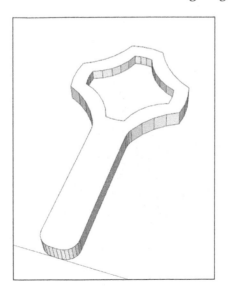

Kim checked the dimensions of the imported wrench right away, to see if they made sense with the size of her GoPro. Fortunately, they were correct. If not, she would have gone back to ensure the units were correct in the Import Options, or scaled the model using the Tape Measure tool, as we discussed in *Chapter 3, From 2D Drawing to 3D Model.*

Since it's harder to work with triangulated models, Kim used the CleanUp extension to remove the unnecessary lines. The link to CleanUp is `http://extensions.sketchup.com/en/content/cleanup%C2%B3`. After running the extension with the **Erase Stray Edges** option checked, the model looks like the following diagram:

To extend the handle, Kim selected all the edges and faces that form the handle end. This is quickly achieved using the **Select** tool and a left-to-right selection box, as shown in the following diagram:

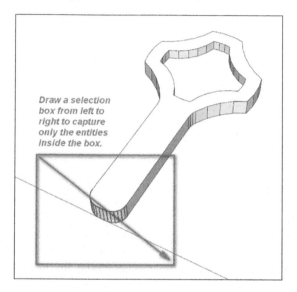

Next, Kim got the **Move** tool and moved the selected entities along the Green (Y) direction until the handle was as long as she wanted. She used the Tape Measure tool to check the length. The following diagram shows the lengthened handle:

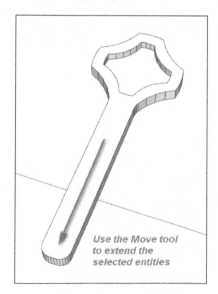

Kim noticed that she can save some weight in the final part by removing some material. Using the **Offset** tool, she creates a new face in the center of the wrench head, as shown in the following diagram:

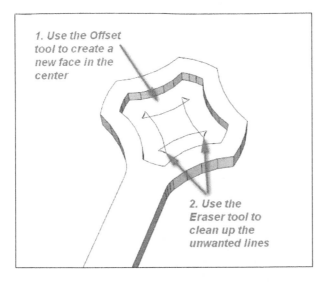

She also used the **Eraser** tool to clean up the extra lines created by the Offset operation, as shown in the following diagram. Leaving the extra lines would prevent her final model from becoming solid.

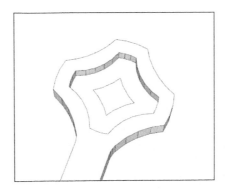

Using the **Push-Pull** tool to push the new face through to the back of the model, a neat hole is formed as shown in the following image.

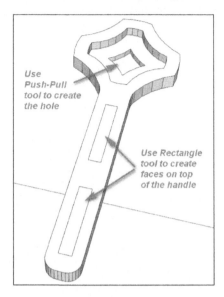

Kim noticed the opportunity to reduce material in the handle as well, so she used the **Rectangle** tool to create two faces on top of the handle, and the Push-Pull tool to create the holes. Kim was happy at this point, and exported the model as an .STL for 3D printing. The following diagram shows how the final model looks:

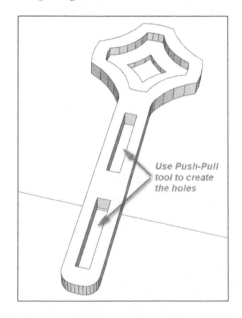

Summary

In this chapter, you have learned some time-saving techniques such as how to save components for later use and where to find 3D printable models online. We have also discussed the editing of downloaded models to perfectly suit your needs.

In the next chapter, we'll design a phone cradle and use iteration to improve the design. We'll also use some advanced modeling techniques to quickly make a complex model.

6
Designing a Phone Cradle

Do you know that feeling when you're watching a video on your smartphone or tablet, and you'd like to place it down, but then it's hard to view, so you end up holding it anyway? Or you're video chatting and need both hands to show how something works, but you can't do so. These are prime examples when a phone cradle can come in handy.

In this chapter, we'll design a cartoon jet phone cradle. This one will be a hit with the kids and a great learning experience for anyone learning how to design for 3D printing.

We will learn about saving time by designing half of a model and then mirroring the remaining part to finish quickly. We will discuss iterating the design, printing text in the model, and how to use the **Intersect with Model** command.

The following is a photo of the completed cradle:

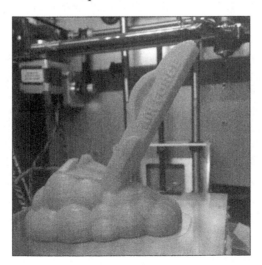

Getting started with a 2D sketch

The vision for this model is a jet taking off at a steep angle, leaving behind clouds of smoke and dust. The clouds will provide a wide base to support the phone in either the portrait or landscape mode.

This model is to be printed on an FFF desktop printer, so we should keep in mind the 45-degree rule and think about minimizing support structures. We can also keep the geometry at a lower resolution to match the capabilities of the printer.

We're going to start by creating a dummy box and drawing on one of its vertical sides, just like we did in *Chapter 4, Understanding Model Resolution*. The following figure shows the profile outlines drawn using the **Line** and **Arc** tools:

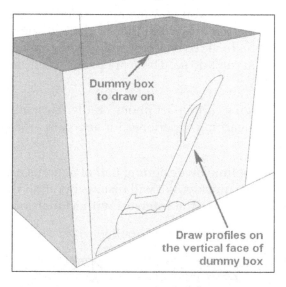

The preceding figure does not show the temporary 45 degree SketchUp guides used to ensure that the overhangs are not too steep. For more details on this technique, refer to *Chapter 4, Understanding Model Resolution*. The cloud and jet profiles are drawn as separate groups and will be joined after pulling into 3D.

Getting to the third dimension

At this point, you'll want to scale your model to size. Using the Tape Measure tool, scale the model to size it to 100 mm in height.

In the following figure, we pull the profiles into 3D, making the cloud base 18 mm thick and the jet 12 mm thick. We join the two groups with the **Outer Shell** tool, ensuring the result is **Solid**:

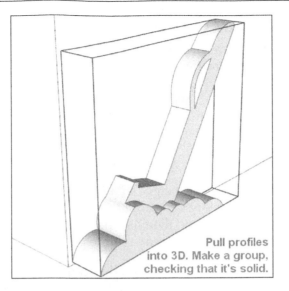

Adding details to make the model interesting

In the following figure, we open the group and draw a wing profile on the existing face of the jet. As the wing is not a true arc, the Bezier Curve Tool extension works best for drawing the curved portion. To minimize the support needed, we'll just pull the wing out by 1.5 mm:

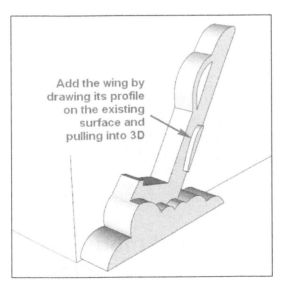

Using the 3D Text tool

Next, we'll add some text with the **3D Text** tool. I wrote **AIR FORCE**, but you can write anything, even your name if you like!

> For 3D printing, non-Serif fonts such as Arial work the best, and bold versions print even better. This is because at small sizes, the thinnest parts of Serif fonts are too thin to be shown in the final print.

In the **Place 3D Text** dialog box, the height should be 5 mm. Make sure the **Extruded** box is checked, and set the thickness to about 0.6 mm. For best results, place the text close to where you want it to go, and then use the **Move** and **Rotate** tools to place it precisely. You'll want to keep the text as a separate group for now.

The 3D text will automatically orient itself to align with whatever face you place it on, and then is *glued* to that plane when you let go of the mouse button. If you're ever trying to move the 3D text and it isn't cooperating, right-click on the text and click on **Unglue**; the text will come free from the original plane.

In the following figure, the 3D text is aligned with the jet and placed near its nose:

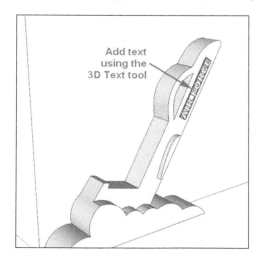

Add text using the 3D Text tool

Mirroring symmetrical models

In symmetrical models such as this one, it is good practice to create half of the model and then mirror the geometry to quickly finish the model. This practice is a huge time saver that we can use now.

In the following figure, we copy the model, scale the copy with a -1 factor using the **Green Scale about Opposite Point** grip, and move it adjacent to the first model, creating a mirrored version of the model and doubling our efforts very quickly. The 3D text must be copied and realigned separately—mirrored text is difficult to read! Another option to mirror the model is to right-click on it and navigate to **Flip Along | Group's Green**, where **Green** refers to the green axis:

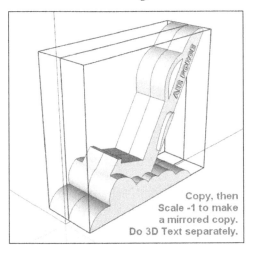

Combining groups with the Outer Shell tool

In the following figure, we copy all the groups to create a historical timeline. Then, we select the 3D text and mirrored groups and use the **Outer Shell** tool to combine everything into one solid model:

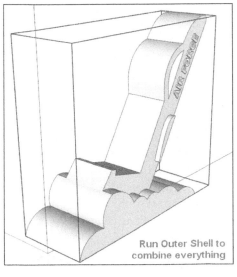

Cutting a slot for the cord

If we think about the final details of the model, we may want to use the cradle with the phone in the portrait mode while charging. On many phones, the charger connects at the bottom of the phone, so we'll need to account for that.

Cutting in a slot will allow us to accommodate the charger and take the phone off the cradle, without unplugging the cord. There are two ways to create a slot through this complex geometry: with the **Solid** tools (Pro version only) or with the **Intersect with Model** command (Make or Pro versions). For now, we'll discuss the **Intersect with Model** command. The process is nearly the same for **Solid** tools but without the tedious cleanup.

We start by creating a box whose width is 13 mm, centered on the group. I chose a width of 13 mm after measuring my phone charger and adding a few millimeter units of wiggle room. The length and height are not important so long as they extend up to or beyond the parts of the model you want to cut.

In the following figure, you can see the orientation of the box that we'll use to create the slot. When complete, the box and everything inside the box will be removed:

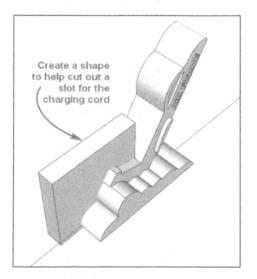

For the **Intersect with Model** command to work, the parts need to be in the same context, which means the parts to be intersected must not be in separate groups. Select the entire box and go to **Edit | Cut** to remove the box and copy it to the clipboard. Open the cradle group and go to **Edit | Paste in Place** to put all geometry in the same context, keeping the placement of the box intact.

[
SketchUp Pro users should group the box to keep the groups separate. To cut the slot, select the box, then go to **Tools | Solid Tools | Subtract**, and then click on the cradle group. The box and everything it contains will be removed, leaving a clean slot.
]

In the following figure, we select everything, then right-click on it and go to **Intersect Faces | With Model**. Depending on how complex your model is, this can take a few seconds or even minutes on really big models:

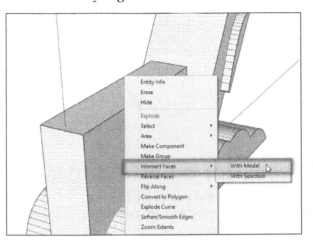

When the operation is complete, you will see that new edges have been created where the intersecting geometry meets, as shown in the next figure. Now, you can start deleting the excess geometry, taking care not to delete anything you want to keep.

This cleanup can be a tedious process—ensure that you get all the extra geometry, but do not delete anything that will make a hole in the good portion of the model. Zooming in close will help you to see tiny extra edges. The Cleanup extension can be of enormous help in this situation since it deletes any stray edges.

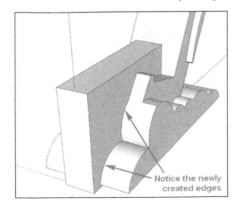

In the following figure, some of the excess geometry has been deleted. Clean up the rest and ensure that you get extra faces and edges that will prevent the model from being solid:

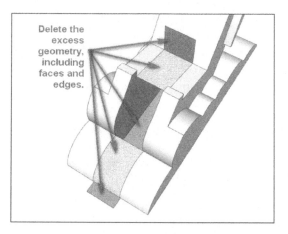

Orienting faces for a perfect model

In the following figure, all the excess geometry has been deleted, which leaves behind a perfect slot. Some faces are reversed but are easily corrected by right-clicking on a white face and then on **Orient Faces**:

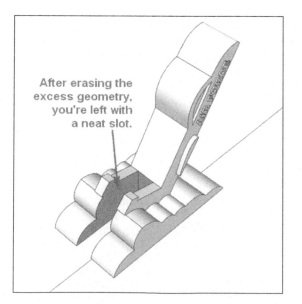

> If the **Orient Faces** command isn't working as you expect it to, the model likely isn't a solid. Check the model for interior faces and delete them.

Exporting the model for printing

In the following figure, all faces are oriented correctly and the model is ready to be printed. Export it for printing, and you're on your way!

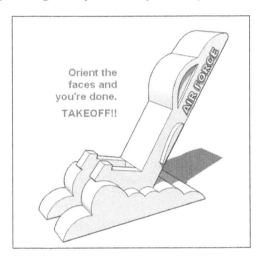

Testing the printed model

The following screenshot shows the printed cradle in use:

After printing the model and testing how it works in practice, I noted the following changes that would improve the design:

- Increasing the height and width of the tabs on the jet's tail fins to keep the phone more stable while in the landscape mode
- Increasing the height of the base so that the charger cord doesn't bend sharply on the table
- Making the jet exhaust clouds more realistic
- Making the plane wings bigger so it's easier to tell what it is

Developing an improved design

Back to SketchUp we go! We'll make the changes and print an improved model. This process of refining the design through a series of iterations is discussed in *Chapter 3, From 2D Drawing to 3D Model*.

Going back in the historical timeline, copy one of the mirrored half groups to rework into the improved design. Use the **Push/Pull** tool and the **Line** tool to make the tabs that hold the phone in place taller and wider. Use the **Push/Pull** tool to pull the bottom face down by another 6 mm, raising the phone up so the charging cord doesn't kink.

For changing the wing shape, push the wing back flush with the plane body, and use the **Bezier** tool to create a new, larger wing profile. Erase the old curve, and use **Push/Pull** to set the new wing back out to 1.5 mm. The larger tabs and the new wing are shown in the following figure:

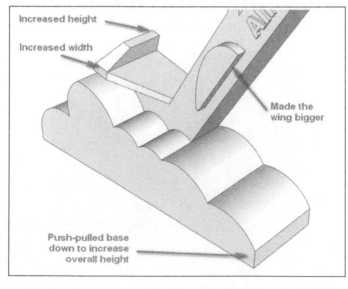

Copying and scaling groups to create a complex shape

For creating more realistic puffy smoke clouds, simply create a sphere and a half-sphere and copy them around the base. You'll want to make sure both the sphere and half-sphere are grouped and solid before making copies of them The half-sphere will create a nice flat base, and the sphere will fill in the top. Use the **Scale** tool to stretch, resize, and deform the copies so that it looks more realistic. Try to keep the 45 degree rule in mind so that the spheres are self-supporting as shown in the following figure. In this figure, all of the spheres and half-spheres are selected so that you can see how many of them make up the new base:

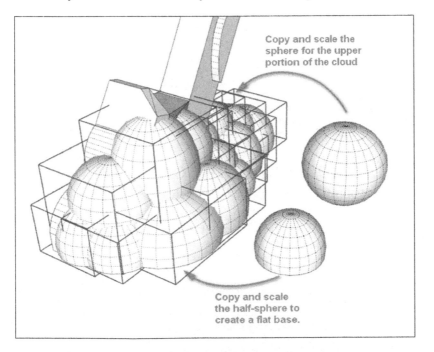

Copy and scale the sphere for the upper portion of the cloud

Copy and scale the half-sphere to create a flat base.

Finally, make a copy of the groups that form your new base. To prevent holes in the model when creating tiny faces in the next step, scale the model up by 100 times using the **Tape Measure** technique described in *Chapter 3, From 2D Drawing to 3D Model*. Use the **Outer Shell** tool to combine everything into one solid group. I found **Outer Shell** to work best when used on only two to three groups at a time. Selecting everything and running the tool often results in a group that s not solid.

Finishing up and printing the new model

Once you have a solid group, make a copy for the historical timeline. Mirror the group, align the 3D text, and combine everything with **Outer Shell**. Cut a slot using the same methods we used in the first iteration of the model. Once that is complete, you should have a model that looks like the following figure:

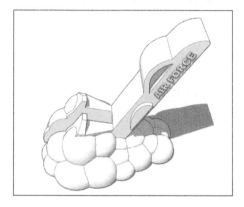

Export the part, and you're ready to print the updated version!

Testing the second iteration

The new part worked much better, comfortably holding the phone and even a small tablet. The increased height prevents the charging cord from kinking, and the larger base looks much better, as shown in the next images. Printing with a red filament enhances the appearance as well!

In the following figure, we see that the same stand can be used for a larger device:

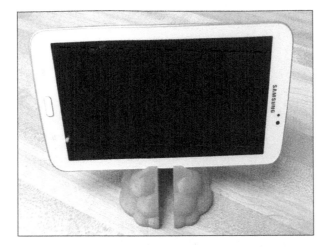

The following figure shows the difference between the two printed designs:

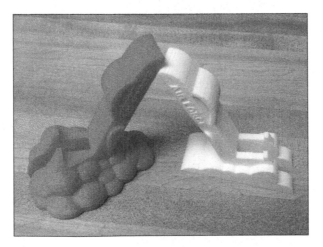

Summary

In this chapter, we learned some advanced modeling techniques such as the **Intersect with Model** command and how to use simple shapes to quickly build up a complex model. By combining these techniques, you can quickly create very complex models. We also used the historical timeline to save time while making a second iteration of the design.

In the next chapter, we'll learn about working with terrain data and how to 3D print models in full color.

7
Importing Terrain and Printing in Color

With geographical data becoming ubiquitous in our digitally connected world, it is now a fairly simple task to use that data in our 3D-printing projects. Include color photos from satellite imagery, use a color-capable printer, and you have a useful scale representation of any corner of the globe.

Commercial grade printers capable of printing thousands of colors in three dimensions are an excellent option for not only terrain models, but also for scale architectural models and visualizing product prototypes. In this chapter, we'll dig right in to see how easy it is to 3D print terrain and multicolored models from SketchUp.

Working with the Google Earth terrain

SketchUp and Google Earth are integrated together so nicely that it really couldn't be easier to import terrain data.

The following are the steps to get Google Earth terrain into SketchUp:

1. First, open SketchUp. Navigate to **File | Geo-Location | Add Location....**

2. A dialog box pops up as shown in the following screenshot. You may need to log in to your Google account to continue. Find the location you are interested in by entering an address, place name, or just navigating the map by panning and zooming:

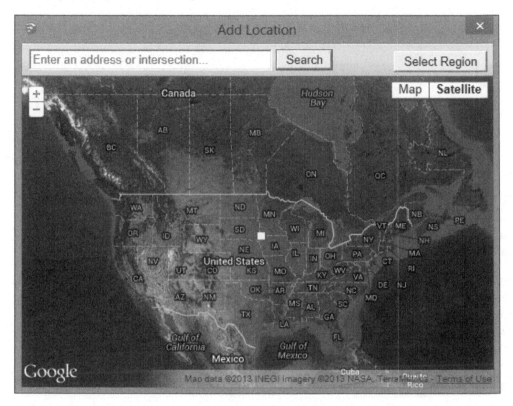

3. Choose a location using the **Select Region** button on the top-right corner of the window. Use the four blue corner pins to fine-tune your selection. The maximum selection size is 2 km (1.2 mi), minimum is 10 m (33 ft).

4. Click on the **Grab** button at the top-right corner of your screen to finish the selection process and import the terrain into SketchUp.

5. You'll see a completely flat satellite image in SketchUp. The terrain is also there, but hidden on a separate layer that is turned off by default. To access it, open the **Layers** window (**Window | Layers**) and check the box next to **Google Earth Terrain**. You can turn off the satellite image by unchecking the box next to **Google Earth Snapshot**.

6. You can see the terrain in 3D now, but it has no thickness. We'll have to add thickness and scale it down to make it 3D printable.

7. The terrain is in a group, but you can't interact with it yet because it's locked. You can tell that it's locked because the group's bounding box is red instead of the usual blue color, and you can't open the group for editing. To unlock the group, simply right-click on the group and click on **Unlock**.

8. All of the lines of the mesh forming the terrain are soft and smooth by default, making it difficult to work with the terrain. To see the lines, either turn on **Hidden Geometry**, as shown in the following screenshot, or unsoften the lines by selecting the group and moving the slider in the **Soften Edges** dialog box (**Window | Soften Edges**) all the way to the left:

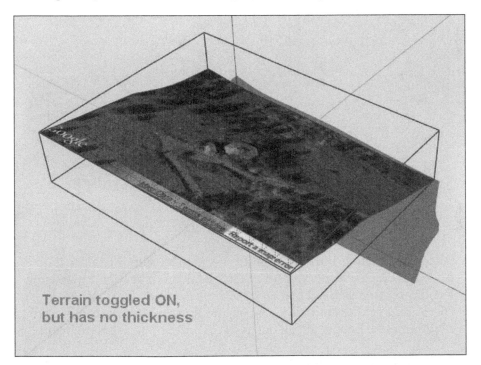

Terrain toggled ON,
but has no thickness

9. Now you need to add thickness to the model. This can be done manually by drawing lines down from each corner and connecting them to form a flat base. Instead, I suggest you use the extension **Add Terrain Skirt** (http://sketchucation.com/forums/viewtopic.php?p=359903#p359903) to complete the task in seconds. Use the **Entity Info** window to ensure the terrain group is **Solid** before continuing. The result of this step is shown in the following screenshot:

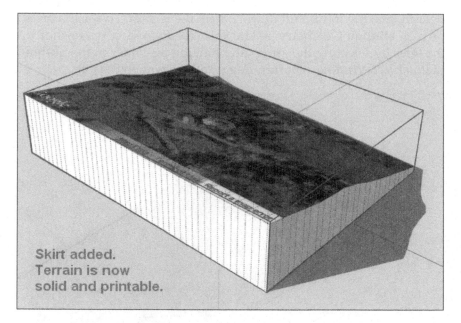

Skirt added.
Terrain is now
solid and printable.

10. Since the terrain is imported at full size, the last step is to scale it down for printing. Use the **Tape Measure** tool to scale your model down using the technique we discussed in *Chapter 3, From 2D Drawing to 3D Model*. Finally, check the thickness of the skirt to ensure that it meets your preferred printer's requirements. Export the model as .stl, and you're ready to print!

This method is a good way to make a terrain model for printing on a desktop FFF printer because the flat base provides a support structure. However, for an industrial printer, you'll want to hollow out the base to use less material. An easy way to do this is with the JointPushPull Interactive extension (http://sketchucation.com/forums/viewtopic.php?p=496773).

JointPushPull can take a collection of connected surfaces and add a precise thickness to them. In our case, we want to keep the skirt walls, but remove most of the mass. To do this, make a copy of the solid terrain model for your historical timeline, then delete the bottom face, as shown in the following screenshot:

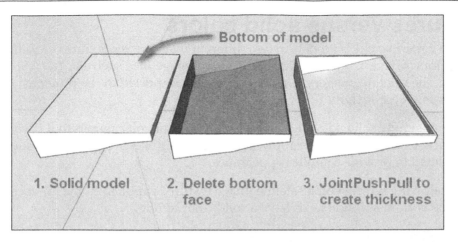

Select all, then use the right-click menu and go to **JointPushPull | Joint Push Pull**. Using the default options, make the terrain and walls 2 mm thick. If you encounter an error, scale the model up by 100 times and then run the operation. You may have to fix some small errors to make the model solid again. In this case, hollowing the model reduced the print material required by 85 percent.

> Google Earth is one source for terrain data, but the quality is low in many places, especially remote locations. There are many more ways to get terrain models including survey data and free online resources. SketchUp Make and SketchUp Pro import .dem files, which is a common format for terrain data.

Since .stl files do not store color data, so far this model can only be printed in a single color. For printing the satellite imagery in color, we need to do some more work on the model.

Printing models with color

It takes a special machine to 3D print in full color, and at this point there are only commercial printers to do the job. This means that unless you're part of a large organization, you'll likely use a print service for printing in color, providing them your model in a format they can use.

Let's discuss how SketchUp processes color data.

Textures versus solid colors

You can color SketchUp models in two different ways—with textures or with plain colors (or a mixture of both). Textures are image files such as .jpg, .png, or .tif. The satellite imagery from the terrain we imported in the previous example is a .jpg texture.

Colors are simply solid colors based on RGB values or color names that cover an entire face. Colors are easier to apply than textures in SketchUp, but need more model detail to provide a similar appearance.

In the following screenshot, a satellite image texture is applied to the top face, while the bottom and side faces have a solid color applied:

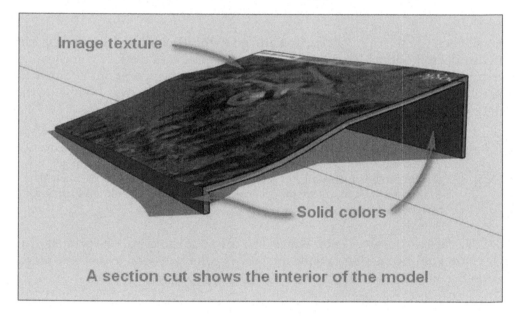

The typical file formats used when 3D printing a color model from SketchUp are .dae and .wrl. SketchUp Pro exports both of these formats. SketchUp Make can only export .dae.

In models using image textures, SketchUp exports the image files separately from the 3D model file. Both image and 3D model files are placed in a ZIP folder to upload to a print service. In models with only colors applied in SketchUp, the 3D model file is all that is required as the color data is stored in the 3D model file.

Be sure to check the print service of your choice before preparing your model, as the file requirements may vary wildly. Some services, such as i.materialise (`http://i.materialise.com/`) and Sculpteo (`http://www.sculpteo.com/`) take SketchUp files directly, which may save you a significant amount of work when preparing the model. Other print services require a ZIP file containing a specific 3D format, such as `.wrl`, and specific image type, such as `.png`. Converting files can be a time-consuming process.

 If you need to convert your files to a format SketchUp does not support, check out the free program, Meshlab (`http://meshlab.sourceforge.net`). With its many import and export options, you will find that it can likely provide a solution for you.

Working with solid colors in SketchUp

To 3D print models with solid colors, be sure all faces have a color applied—do not leave any faces with the default material. Likewise, check to make sure that there are no colors applied to the back of the faces, as this may cause unwanted conflict with the printer. To remove color from a back face, simply paint the back face with the default material.

View the model in monochrome (**View | Face Style | Monochrome**), which turns the colors off and allows you to ensure that all faces are oriented correctly. If any faces are reversed, right-click on that face and click on **Reverse Faces** to correct the problem. For more about face orientation, refer to *Chapter 2, Setting Up SketchUp for 3D Printing*.

That's pretty much it. Now simply export the model in a format compatible with the printer, and you're ready to roll.

Working with textures in SketchUp

The basic rules for working with solid colors apply to textured SketchUp models as well; avoid conflict with front and back face materials, and use Monochrome to check for correct face orientation.

Sometimes you may need to scale and rotate textures for precise placement. In this case, you use the texturing tools by right-clicking on the screen and navigating to **Texture | Position**, which will only work when clicking on a face with an image texture applied.

Exporting the model for color printing

If your print provider doesn't take SketchUp files directly for printing, the final step is to export the model. In my experience, the file type that seems to work best with most service providers is `.dae`.

Using the **Tape Measure** tool, make sure the model is at the correct scale. Delete your historical timeline and everything else in the SketchUp file except for the model to be printed.

You may want to create a folder specifically for this export so that the 3D model and corresponding image file can be found easily. Finally, to export the model, go to **File | Export | 3D Model...**, and then click on **COLLADA file (*.dae)** from the drop-down menu at the bottom of the screen.

When uploading to your print provider, make a ZIP file containing the DAE and JPG files as shown in the following screenshot. Upload the ZIP file to your print provider, and you'll be holding a color print shortly.

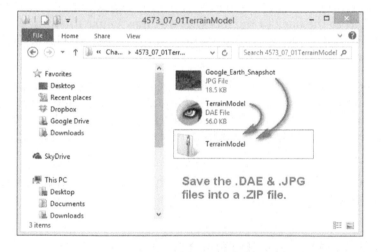

Summary

SketchUp integration with Google Earth makes it very easy to import terrain data. We learned how to make the terrain 3D printable by adding a skirt and scaling to size. We learned about an extension that allows us to quickly create a hollow model, reducing the model volume by 85 percent. We discussed the difference between solid colors and textures in SketchUp, and how that affects packaging the model for the printer.

In the next chapter, we'll learn about preparing architectural models for printing.

8
Modeling Architecture for 3D Printing

Architectural rendering is SketchUp's forte. With the many styles available in SketchUp, there is no easier program to create beautiful visualizations. With extensions and external programs that work with SketchUp files, you can create photorealistic renders and augmented reality models. As nice as these outputs are, they are still constrained to the two-dimensional confines of paper and digital screen.

Scale architectural models are incredibly useful in a way that 2D representations simply can't match. Historically, scale models were painstakingly made by hand from foam core board, wood, and the patience of an angel. More recently, laser cutters have made the tedious job of cutting easier, but designing the digital files and assembling the parts is still time consuming and rarely can the SketchUp files be used without major rework.

3D printing alleviates many of these problems. By starting with an existing architectural model, you can quickly make a 3D printable model with minimal effort. What's more, building on the techniques we discussed in *Chapter 7, Importing Terrain and Printing in Color*, you can even print scale architectural models in full color!

In this chapter, we will cover some advanced techniques that may be difficult if you haven't used SketchUp much. If you have trouble following along, please refer to *Appendix, Resources for Your 3D Printing Success*, for SketchUp training resources.

Using SketchUp for 3D printing versus rendering

Many of the requirements of a 3D printable model do not apply when modeling SketchUp models intended for visualizations. Models can be (and often are) designed as quickly as possible, with no wall thickness, with intersecting geometry, and without separate groups or components. A quick look at random models downloaded from the 3D warehouse can confirm this. While these models work just fine for their intended purpose, printing them in 3D proves tricky.

Another problem occurs when scaling the model down. Using the **Tape Measure** or **Scale** tool, you can easily shrink a model to fit in a 3D printer, but even well-built architectural models not designed with 3D printing in mind will need some rework. Small features in a rendering model such as door knobs, window trim, and window grills (muntin bars), will be much too small for the printer.

For example, a half-inch wide window grill scaled at 1:48 to fit on a small printer will only be 0.2 mm wide—much too small for most printers and certainly not strong enough to withstand handling. A good rule of thumb for most printers is not to include freestanding features smaller than 1-2 mm.

Case study – 3D printing a model designed for rendering

The small house movement (http://en.wikipedia.org/wiki/Small_house_movement) is becoming popular with people who want to live simply and have less impact on the environment. Also called micro homes, tiny cabins, and a variety of other creative names, these dwellings are often built on a trailer for portability.

One of the clients from my architectural rendering business is a tiny cabin designer and builder. Jim Wilkins, owner of Tiny Green Cabins, will send me a hand-sketched design with measurements, which I'll model in SketchUp and render to create photorealistic images that he uses to sell the finished cabins. For folks who want to build the cabin themselves, Jim sells a set of construction plans created in Layout, which is a part of the SketchUp Pro package. In this chapter, we'll learn the steps necessary to convert the actual model I used for rendering a tiny cabin into a 3D-printable model as shown in the following image. You may follow along with an architectural model of your own, or one from the 3D Warehouse. This process will be similar for many architectural models:

Examining the original model

The following screenshot shows the original model that was made for rendering:

In the following screenshot, we turn the textures off (**View | Face Style | Monochrome**), so the back faces will show in orange. We can use the **Section Plane** tool to look inside the model. The **Section Plane** tool creates a nondestructive *cut* in the model, allowing you to look or work inside an enclosed space. By right-clicking on the section plane, it can be turned on or off, hidden, and reversed.

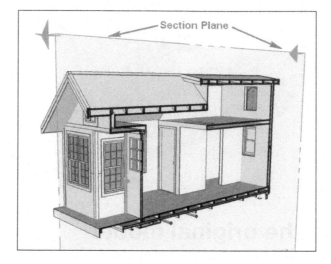

At first glance, we can see numerous issues with 3D printing the model. Because we're using the style we created in *Chapter 2, Setting Up SketchUp for 3D Printing*, we can see numerous back faces showing in orange that will need to be fixed. The panes of glass have no thickness, the cabin is a mass of separate nested groups and components of which many are not solid, and some features are too small to print. For this model, I will not be printing the trailer wheels and hitch, which will simplify the process and make the final print more durable.

For the first print, let's design for FFF printing. I'm going to be using my Solidoodle desktop 3D printer that has a maximum build area of 6" x 6" x 6" (150 mm x 150 mm x 150 mm). The overall length of the cabin is 24" (7.3 m), so with a little simple math (or trial and error) I know that at 1:48 scale, the model will just fit on my printer.

> Here's a trick to quickly resize a model to any scale; for example, 1:48 — draw a line in empty space 48 mm long. Using the **Tape Measure** tool, first click on one end then the other end of the line, type 1 mm and hit *Enter*. SketchUp will ask if it's OK to resize the model, just click on **Yes** and voila, the model is scaled precisely. This works with any unit of measurement because you're changing the 48-unit-long line to 1 unit long and the rest of the model is scaled to match. If you have trouble with some of the imported components not scaling to match, simply enclose the entire model in a new group before scaling.

Taking into account the requirements of FFF printing, we know that the eaves will not print without support. To minimize support, we'll print the roof separately and since the roof has two separate pitches, we'll print it in two pieces. For the windows, we'll remove the glass and print just the grills for a window-like effect.

Planning the model

Trying to fix this model by making all the components solid, beefing up the thin features, and repairing the windows is doable, but would be a tedious and mentally painful process. There are extensions that attempt to automate the process, but I haven't found any that really work well. One approach that seems to work best is to use the original as a guide while constructing a new, printable model around it.

In this process, we'll create solid shapes that are of the correct thickness for printing, and assemble them like LEGO pieces into the exact shape needed. For features too small to print, we'll exaggerate their size to make them large enough for printing, or simply eliminate them. Using the **Outer Shell** command, at the end we'll combine all the pieces into a solid, printable model.

Thinking about the minimum features for this printer, let's plan ahead to print this model in full color. To save time then, we'll make sure this model works for both an FFF printer and a full color printer as much as possible. In the end, we'll have one model for each type of printing, each tweaked with the necessary requirements.

After checking the requirements for full color material (`http://i.materialise.com/materials/multicolor/design-guide`), we can see that the minimum wall thickness is 1.5-2.0 mm, and minimum detail is 0.8-1.0 mm. FFF printers can also work within these guidelines, so we'll keep them in mind while modeling.

The full color printer is powder-based, so we'll want to make the model hollow to save on material costs.

Using groups and layers to organize the model

The first thing to do is group the entire cabin and place it on its own layer so that we can quickly hide and show it as needed. To do this, press *Ctrl + A* to select all of the geometry in the model, then navigate to **Edit | Make Group**. Open the **Layers** dialog box by navigating to **Window | Layers**, and clicking on the plus icon to add a layer. Name it `0 - original` (if there other layers in the model, the 0 makes the new layer stay at the top of the layer list, so you can find it easily). Select the group, and in the **Entity Info** window, set the layer to `0 - original`. Now, we can toggle visibility of the original model using the **Layers** window.

The following screenshot shows this process:

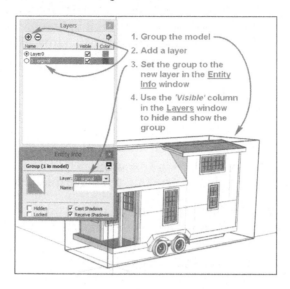

The **Hide** and **Unhide** commands can also be used to toggle visibility of groups in the model. Setting these commands to keyboard shortcuts can dramatically speed up your workflow.

Creating a standard wall thickness

Let's begin modeling! We'll use the trailer bed as a base to provide most of the structural support, so let's make it 5 mm thick. Off to the side, draw a rectangle larger than the trailer, extrude it by 5 mm, and make it a group. Paint it with a bright color to distinguish it from the rest of the model in the next steps, as shown in the following screenshot:

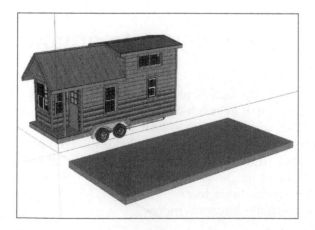

Using the **Move** tool, grab the top-front corner of the new trailer bed, and place it on the top-front corner of the original trailer. Zoom in closely during this operation to place the geometry precisely as shown in the following screenshot. Notice how the top is aligned, but the new geometry hangs lower to increase the thickness of the trailer bed for strength in the printed product. We can tell the top faces are aligned because of the visible "Z-fighting", which happens when two faces share the same plane and both colors fight for visibility as the model is orbited.

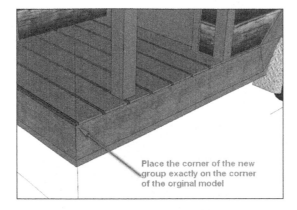

Place the corner of the new group exactly on the corner of the orginal model

Orbit to the other side of the model where the new geometry is much too large. This is easily fixed using the **Scale** tool. Select the new group, click on the **Scale** tool and using only the center-most scale grip on one side, squash the group until it's of the correct size. Using the center-most grip will scale the group along one axis at a time, as shown in the following screenshot. The **Push/Pull** tool will work for this operation as well, but using the **Scale** tool saves the extra steps of opening and closing the group:

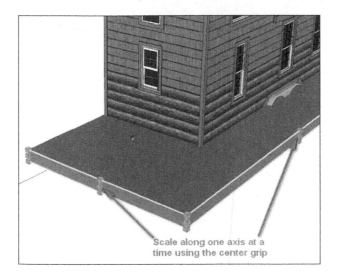

Scale along one axis at a time using the center grip

Use inferencing with the **Scale** tool to align the new group with the original model as shown in the following screenshot, and then repeat for the last side of the new trailer bed:

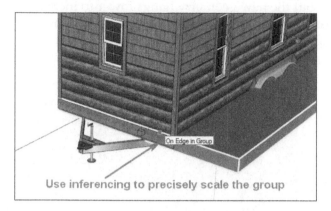

Use inferencing to precisely scale the group

Let's make the exterior walls 3 mm thick. Create a rectangular box 3 mm wide, off to one side, as shown in the following screenshot. Make the box into a group. By copying this group and using it to create new walls in place of the existing model, we'll ensure an even 3 mm wall thickness throughout the model:

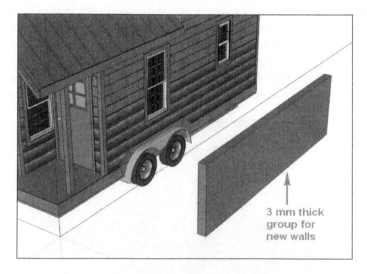

3 mm thick group for new walls

Turn off the original model layer so that it doesn't interfere, and position the new wall on the new trailer bed. Turning the original model layer on and off as needed and using the **Scale** tool just as we did with the trailer bed, align the new wall with the original as shown in the following screenshot. Scale only one direction (length or height) at a time and never along the thickness. This way the walls will all be of a uniform 3 mm thickness:

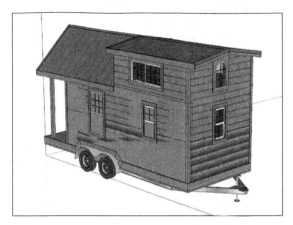

Copy the new wall to the opposite side of the cabin and repeat the process for each of the remaining walls. Notice that we *copy* the first wall to create the second, rather than drawing another from scratch. Copy and rotate the first wall by 90 degrees for the end walls.

 The most important thing at this point is to be precise in making sure all the walls meet at their respective corners. The walls can overlap, but if there is a gap and the walls do not touch, the **Outer Shell** operation and/or the final print will fail.

Editing wall panels to add details

To make the peaked gables on the end walls, scale the end wall up to the top of the peak, open that group for editing, and draw lines for the peaks, as shown in the following screenshot. Push-pull the excess material away to finish up.

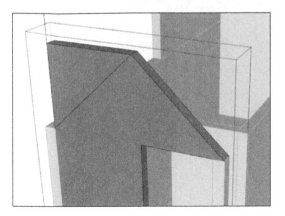

When this step is complete, the walls should look like the following screenshot. Windows and doors will be cut in the next step.

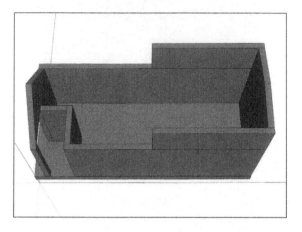

To cut the windows, turn the original model layer on and create a guideline perpendicular to the wall. Use the **Move** tool along with *CTRL* to copy and place two guidelines on each window at opposite corners. This creates two points piercing the new wall that we can use to draw a rectangle directly on the new wall and push-pull it by creating a window as shown in the following screenshot:

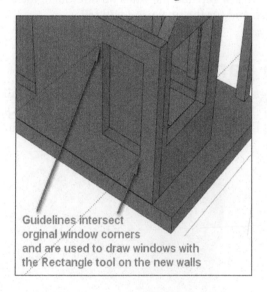

Guidelines intersect orginal window corners and are used to draw windows with the Rectangle tool on the new walls

Adding the window grills

The next step is to place the window grills. This is one feature that needs to be exaggerated in order to print correctly. At a 1:48 scale, the thickness of the grills in the original model is only 0.2 mm thick—much too thin for printing on the machines we chose. Since the grills are just spanning a short distance, the minimum recommended wall thickness of 1.5 mm should work fine. Draw a square 1.5 mm x 1.5 mm, extrude it up about the height of a window, and make it a group as shown in the following screenshot:

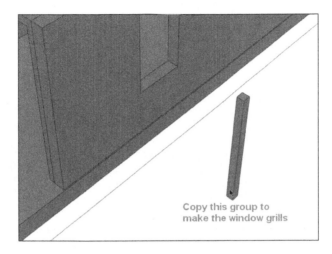

Copy this group to
make the window grills

Move it into position, inferencing the midpoint of the grill group to the midpoint on the window. Scale only along the long, vertical axis as needed to fit in the window. Make a copy and rotate it 90 degrees to create the horizontal portion, and then copy these two groups to the other windows, centering them as you go. You'll want to be careful to always make sure the window grill groups are abutting or intersecting with the wall groups, leaving no gaps that will cause problems with printing.

The following screenshot shows what the walls look like with all the windows and doors cut out, and the window grills in place:

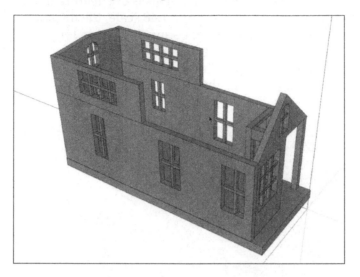

Adding interior walls

The interior walls and loft of the cabin are added using the same method we used for the exterior. Since these walls will not be handled as much, they don't need to be as strong, so we can make them thinner — 2 mm will be enough. The interior is shown in the following screenshot:

Modeling the roof

The next step is modeling the roof. First, draw the roof profile, ensuring a minimum wall thickness of 1.5 mm in all places. In the following screenshot, the overall thickness is 4 mm so that near the eaves the thickness is sufficient. In the following screenshot, notice the 0.2 mm clearance between the eaves and walls, so the separate roof isn't too tight to place on the top:

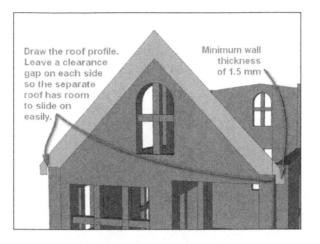

Push-pull the roof to match the length of the original model. Perform the same steps for the upper roof, and make the vertical walls to connect the space between the upper and lower roof, drawing each portion in a separate group, but combining the vertical walls and the steep roof with the **Outer Shell** tool.

In the following screenshot, you can see the completed roof assembly, with the rest of the model hidden:

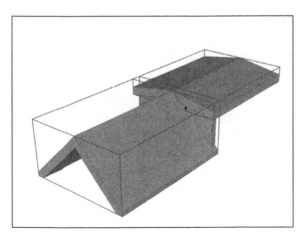

The two roof pitches are kept separate for printing on the FFF printer. Since the two roofs overlap in the center of the cabin, I used the **Subtract** tool in SketchUp Pro to cut away the portion that was overlapping. You can perform the same action using the **Intersect with Model** command in SketchUp Make. For more information on the **Intersect with Model** command, please refer to *Chapter 6, Designing a Phone Cradle*.

Orienting the parts for printing

The model is now nearly complete. In the following screenshot, notice how the roofs are positioned for easy printing with no support. The vertical walls connecting the upper and lower roofs are able to be placed flat on the print bed, while the rest of the roof geometry is self-supporting:

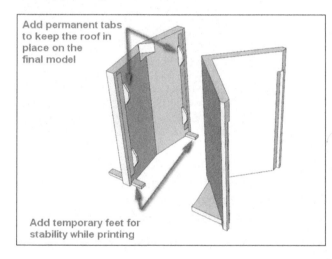

While the roofs are in the printing position, we can add more features. The shallow roof on the left has little surface area but a relatively great height. Tall, thin features like these can easily be knocked over by the print head during printing. By adding temporary feet, we can ensure that the roof will be stable for printing. These feet can be cut off with a knife after printing.

Another feature we can add now is stabilizing tabs to the shallow roof. The steep roof has ridges that can grip the top of the walls after printing, but the shallow roof does not have much to keep it from sliding off the walls. By adding tabs as shown in the previous screenshot, the roof is stabilized and the tabs are hidden on the finished model. Adding them while in the printing position allows us to be sure the tabs meet the 45-degree rule for printing overhangs without support.

Moving on toward the interior, we can see the loft creates a large overhang that will require a lot of support if printed in place. Select the interior walls and loft, and connect them into one solid with the **Outer Shell** tool.

By keeping the interior walls and loft separate from the rest of the model, we can print them upside down so that no support is needed, as shown in the following screenshot:

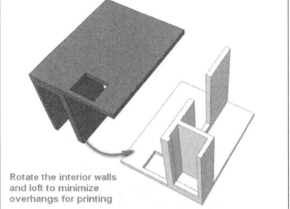

Rotate the interior walls and loft to minimize overhangs for printing

The four sections of the model can be printed all at once on the printer with no extra support, and assembled immediately afterward with little to no hand work. The only thing remaining is to combine the walls, base, and window grill groups into one solid for printing. As usual, make a copy of everything for your historical timeline before performing the operation. This way, if you need to go back and edit a particular part of the model, the separate groups make the job much easier.

In the following screenshot, the model is completed and ready to export for printing on a desktop printer:

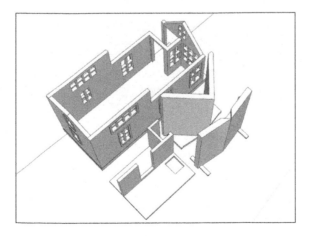

Printing the model and bonus commentary

In the following three images, you can see the final printed model. All of the parts feel strong, and they fit together well. As a communication tool, this model will definitely work well:

The interior walls and loft group are snapped tightly into place. As an afterthought, I could have printed the interior and the walls with the rest of the model, and printed just the loft floor separately.

You probably noticed that the windows' grills are missing—well, after printing the model twice without good results, I cut them out with a knife.

Remember how you learned tall, thin prints don't work well? A good example of that occurrence is shown in the following image, right after the printer finished making a second print of the cabin:

Notice how some of the windows look fine, but most of the vertical parts of the grills are missing. The tall thin posts easily get knocked over when the print head passes over them. On this second print, I added another horizontal bar across the tall windows to shorten the vertical bars. I also increased their thickness from 1.5 mm to 2 mm, but that still didn't work well. Any larger, and the grill would fill up too much of the window, so I felt cutting them out was the best option.

The tall, thin post on the corner of the porch proved troublesome for the same reason on the first print. Thickening it up to 4.5 mm worked well on the second print.

To save material, I reduced the base thickness to 2.5 mm in the second print from 5 mm in the original model. It still has plenty of strength, but saved significant printing time and material.

Printing this model challenged my skills on the 3D printer. Operating the printer is an art in itself, and having owned my own printer for only a few short months at the time of this writing, I have not learned all the printer settings to tweak for different situations. It is possible by changing some settings that even the windows would have printed well on this model.

Statistics are fun, right? The following are the vitals for this model:

• Printed in ABS plastic with a heated bed and enclosure

• 8 hours of printing time for a complete set of parts

• $2.25 of material, not including the re-print

This troubleshooting and reprinting experience is typical in home 3D printers, and is the reason why sending a model off to a print service can be a much better use of a designer's time. In the next section, this is exactly what we'll do!

Preparing the model for full color printing

To get the full benefit of the original textured model, we can print this model in color using the same textures applied to render the model. Refer to *Chapter 7, Importing Terrain and Printing in Color*, for requirements of printing in color.

Because the color printers are powder-based, the prints are self-supporting and we can combine the parts into two solids. We want the roof to be removable so that the interior layout is visible, as shown in the following screenshot. By combining the two roof parts together, and the interior and exterior walls together, we can minimize the post-printing assembly work.

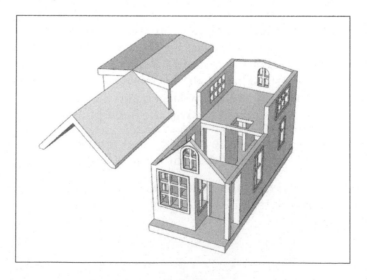

Looking at the requirements for this material from the print service i.materialise `http://i.materialise.com/materials/multicolor/design-guide`, we can see that multiple parts are allowed in one print file, so this approach will work fine.

The i.materialise service is a good choice for beginners printing color SketchUp models because they accept the `.SKP` format directly. Other print services may require you to convert color models to `.DAE` or `.WRL`, and to combine all the textures in the file into a single texture map containing all of the textures in a model.

The next step will be to apply textures to the new model. Since image textures in SketchUp have a real-world scale, for texturing, it's best to scale the model back up to life size. Turning on the original model to use as a reference, apply textures and colors to the model. In this step, SketchUp's (**projected textures**) may not work for 3D printing.

> Use the eyedropper **Sample** tool to quickly select a material from the original model. To use the eyedropper, select the **Paint Bucket** tool, then hold down the *Alt* key [Windows] or *Command* key [Mac] and select the material you want. Release the modifier key to paint the new model with that material.

To break a large face such as the floor into multiple textures, simply draw a line across the face where you want to change the texture. The line must be connected to edges on both ends to break the face. Now you can apply a different material on each side of the line.

When you complete texturing, every front face should have a texture applied, and no back face should be textured. To easily check this, change the style to show a bright color on the front face, as we discussed for back faces in *Chapter 2, Setting Up SketchUp for 3D Printing*. If you see an untextured face, this is the time to fix it. Use **Section Plane** to check the interior walls.

To check the back faces, simply reverse all of the faces; triple-click on the faces to select all faces, right-click on the model, and click on **Reverse Faces**. While all the faces are still selected, apply the default material to them to quickly ensure that there are no unwanted textures. Applying the default texture to the back faces will not interfere with the colored textures on the front faces. Now, you can right-click on the faces and click on **Reverse Faces** a second time to return the textured faces facing out.

Repeat this process for both the roof and walls' groups, making the model look like the following screenshot:

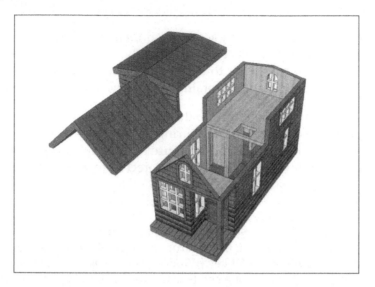

Check the model one last time to be sure both groups are solid, and fix them if necessary. Now scale the model back down to printing size. Save the model as a new file, and delete everything but the two groups that will be printed. Since i.materialise accepts SketchUp files directly, this is the model we'll upload for printing.

Orienting the parts for printing

The final step is to make the model compact by positioning the two groups as near to each other as possible, minimizing their combined bounding box. (A bounding box is the smallest imaginary box the model will fit into.) This will save space in the printing tray, and the print service will give us a better price. We don't want the parts to touch or intersect though, or else the printer will fuse the two parts together.

Placing the roof in position over the walls will make the smallest bounding box for this model. The design guidelines specify a minimum of 0.4 mm clearance between two parts to keep them separate. To be safe, let's move the roof 2 mm up and 2 mm forward toward the entrance door to keep it separate from the walls, as shown in the following screenshot:

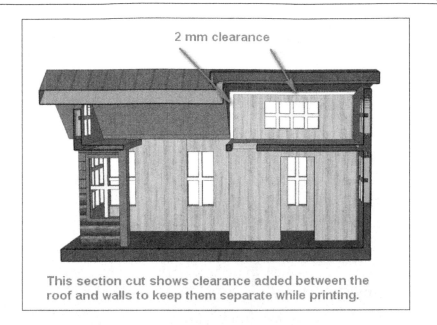

2 mm clearance

This section cut shows clearance added between the roof and walls to keep them separate while printing.

Printing from i.materialise

You can upload the model to the i.materialise website (`http://i.materialise.com/`), or use their extension (`http://extensions.sketchup.com/en/content/3d-print-service`) to upload the model directly from inside SketchUp. If you have any trouble during the upload and ordering process, you can e-mail customer service for help.

The model is ready to print via i.materialise!

Printing from Shapeways

To print this model via Shapeways, we'll have to export the model as `.DAE` or `.WRL`. Refer to *Chapter 7, Importing Terrain and Printing in Color*, for a step-by-step process.

More details about Shapeways requirements for color printing can be found at `https://www.shapeways.com/tutorials/exporting_to_vrml_and_x3d_for_color_printing`.

The full-color printed cabin

To print this model, I chose Shapeways for faster service and a slightly better price. The model arrived in about two weeks, and I could not be happier with how it turned out. The finish is somewhat rough, like a sugar cube. The colors are bright and vibrant, but I'm especially pleased with how the window grills look in the following two images:

In the following image, you can see the crisp detail of the ridge seating the base of the roof to the walls. The fit is excellent, and makes the cabin look like one piece when in place:

It's nice to place an order and get back a perfect model, printed by professionals. This approach allows you as a designer to focus on making models rather than troubleshooting failed prints. Of course, if you like the challenge of operating a 3D printer, there is nothing wrong with that!

Summary

In this chapter, you learned how to use an existing architectural SketchUp model as a template for creating a 3D-printable model. You also learned about how to split a model into parts to minimize support structures on a desktop FFF printer, and some of the adventures of trying to print the model.

We also discussed printing the models in full color from two different print services, and how your approach differs for each. Sending out a model to be printed by professionals allows you as a designer to focus on modeling and not worry about 3D printer failures.

In the *Appendix*, *Resources for Your 3D Printing Success*, you'll find a troubleshooting guide that lists solutions to problems that prevent your models from becoming solid. There is also a resource list of programs that will help you with 3D printing your SketchUp models.

Resources for Your 3D Printing Success

In this reference section, you'll find fast answers to common problems and questions that I had while learning how to model in SketchUp, and while learning the specifics of 3D printing SketchUp models. There is also a curated list of my favorite programs and websites used in relation to 3D printing.

Troubleshooting nonsolid models

These are some common problems that may prevent your model from being solid. Use the Solid Inspector extension to help highlight these problems.

 In a solid model, every edge is bounded by exactly two faces. Any more, and there will be internal faces. Any less, and there will be a hole.

The following troubleshooting guide table is meant to be printed out for quick reference when you need it:

Problems	Solution
Intersecting or overlapping faces	Use the **Intersect with Model** command to create edges at the intersections, and then delete the internal faces. If the intersecting faces are separate solid groups, use the **Outer Shell** tool to combine them.
Holes in the model	Draw a line over one of the edges bounding the hole to form a face. If this doesn't work, use the **Line** tool to connect the hole's open edges. Since a triangle shape will always make a face, try stitching the hole together with triangles.
	If the edges are very small (less than approximately 1 mm long), you will need to scale the model up to fill in the holes.
Duplicate faces	This problem can be tricky to spot because the problem area highlighted by Solid Inspector looks perfectly fine. It happens when multiple faces form in one place. Simply select and delete the faces one-by-one until you make a hole, then **Undo** one step to replace the last face.
	Making a copy of the model with the **Move** tool also corrects the problem, and may be faster for models with many duplicate faces.
Group inside a group	Nested groups or components will not be identified as solids by SketchUp, even if all the other requirements are met. Solid Inspector does not highlight this problem either.
	The solution is to move the nested group outside the context of the main group using the **Cut** and **Paste in place** commands under the **Edit** menu.
Internal faces	Any geometry that is inside the solid model, not a part of the surface, will prevent the model from being a solid. Select and delete this geometry.
	To see the inside of a model, you can use the **Section Plane** tool. Another good method is to cut a portion of the model, and then use **Paste in place** to replace the **Cut** geometry when you're done working inside.
	On models with curved surfaces, use the **Soften Edges** dialog box to make the surface look smooth. If there is a hard edge visible where the model should be smooth, check that area for internal faces.

Problems	Solution
Reversed faces	Reversed faces will not prevent SketchUp from showing a model as solid, but you'll have trouble trying to print the model. Right-click, then click on **Reverse faces** to correct this problem.
	If there are many reversed faces, right-click on a front face, then click on **Orient Faces** to fix all of them at once. If the **Orient Faces** command doesn't work, you probably have internal faces in the model that need to be removed.
Stray lines	Stray lines are lines connected at only one end. Simply erase them, or use the Cleanup extension to automatically remove them.

SketchUp extensions

Extensions, also called plugins, extend SketchUp's functionality and can be found in many places on the Web.

Where to find extensions online

The following websites are the best places to download extensions:

- Extensions Warehouse at `http://extensions.sketchup.com/` is the official extensions site. It is also available directly inside SketchUp and can be found by navigating to **Window | Extensions Warehouse**.

- SketchUcation Plugin Store at `http://sketchucation.com/resources/plugin-store-download`. This is an extension for downloading and managing extensions, having the largest collection of SketchUp plugins online, with instant install, plugin sorting, and more useful features.

- Smustard at `http://www.smustard.com/`. It is a collection of free and for-pay plugins.

Extensions and plugins mentioned in the book

The following extensions and plugins are mentioned in this book:

- SketchUp STL at `http://extensions.sketchup.com/en/content/sketchup-stl` converts SketchUp models into the common `.stl` format for 3D printing

- Solid Inspector at `http://extensions.sketchup.com/en/content/solid-inspector` checks for errors preventing solid groups and components

- CleanUp[3] at http://extensions.sketchup.com/en/content/ cleanup%C2%B3 automatically deletes stray lines and performs other tedious tasks

- Import DXF at http://sketchucation.com/forums/viewtopic. php?f=323&t=31186 imports existing artwork in .DXF format

- Edge Tools[2] at https://extensions.sketchup.com/en/content/ edge-tools[2] cleans up imported .DXF and .DWG files

- Make Faces at http://www.smustard.com/script/MakeFaces fills in imported linework with faces for pushing/pulling into 3D

- Roundcorner at http://sketchucation.com/forums/viewtopic. php?t=20485 is used to add fillets to your 3D model, making the corners rounded

- BezierSpline at http://sketchucation.com/forums/viewtopic. php?t=13563 is used to make complex curves

- Joint Push Pull Interactive at http://sketchucation.com/forums/ viewtopic.php?p=496773 is used to make wall thickness; it works best on models of simple to medium complexity

- Add Terrain Skirt at http://sketchucation.com/forums/viewtopic. php?p=359903#p359903 quickly adds a flat base to terrain models, making them solid for printing

- i.materialise 3D Print Service at http://extensions.sketchup.com/en/ content/3d-print-service uploads a model directly from SketchUp to i.materialise

More useful extensions

The following extensions are also useful:

- Curviloft at http://forums.sketchucation.com/viewtopic.php?t=28586 is used to create complex curved surfaces.

- Bounding box at http://extensions.sketchup.com/en/content/draw-boundingbox draws faces on the bounding box of a group or component. It is useful for aligning odd-shaped objects.

- Artisan priced $39 at http://artisan4sketchup.com/ adds subdivision capabilities inside SketchUp for organic modeling.

SketchUp training

If you're new to SketchUp, use the following resources that I referred to when learning how to model:

- SketchUp's official training [http://www.sketchup.com/learn]; free videos, downloadable step-by-step tutorials, and more, directly from the SketchUp team.

- *Google SketchUp 8 for Dummies, Wiley Publishing* at http://www.aidanchopra.com/book-info, written by one of the SketchUp team members for SketchUp 8 in an easy-to-follow format. The vast majority of the book still applies to current SketchUp versions.

- SketchUp School at http://www.go-2-school.com/, video training from experts, also available for free on YouTube at http://www.youtube.com/user/4sketchupgo2school.

Companion programs for 3D printing

The following programs work with 3D models, providing functionality that SketchUp lacks:

- Netfabb Basic at http://www.netfabb.com/basic.php is a free program for manipulating and fixing errors in STL files.

- Netfabb Cloud at https://netfabb.azurewebsites.net/ is a powerful free STL repairing hosted online. Use this to clean up models and fix errors such as missing faces, and internal geometry.

- Meshlab at http://meshlab.sourceforge.net/ is used to convert many files to import into SketchUp or convert models exported from SketchUp.

3D model repositories

The following websites host models that others have made. Download them and modify for your needs. A huge time-saver if you can find a model close to what you need!

- Thingiverse (http://www.thingiverse.com/) is the largest collection of files for 3D printing online

- SketchUp 3D Warehouse (https://3dwarehouse.sketchup.com/) is a vast collection of SketchUp models, most of which are not printable without making them solid

- GrabCAD (https://grabcad.com/) are engineering grade models, most of which will need conversion to allow import to SketchUp

3D print services

If you don't own a printer, you'll need a print service to have models made for you. Even if you do own a printer, you may need a model printed in a material you don't have access to. There are a couple of different business models that print services use.

Industrial services with a shop platform

The following services allow designers to order high quality models as well as sell designs to the public. The printing and customer service is fulfilled by the print service. Designers are paid if someone purchases their model.

- Shapeways at `http://www.shapeways.com/` usually has the best prices and awesome customer service. It has offices in New York and the Netherlands.

- i.materialise at `http://i.materialise.com/` has an excellent selection of materials, good SketchUp support, fast priority service, and cool contests. It is based in Belgium.

- Sculpteo at `http://www.sculpteo.com/en/` can print SketchUp files, offers fast printing times, and has innovative tools for designers. It is based in France.

- Kraftwurx at `http://www.kraftwurx.com/` has a huge variety of materials available, by far the largest selection—platinum and many more. It is based in Texas, USA, with printing hubs around the world.

Crowdsourced print services

The following websites act as a platform allowing anyone to list their printer and accept and fulfill printing jobs. You can usually find a local printer using one of these services. Most printer listings are for small desktop printers, but there are also many small businesses with industrial printers and engineering staff on hand to provide personalized help.

- MakeXYZ (`http://makexyz.com/`)
- 3DHubs (`http://www.3dhubs.com/`)

Contact me

I sincerely hope this book has brought you value on your SketchUp to 3D printing journey. If there is anything else at all that I can help you with, please e-mail me directly at `marcus@denali3ddesign.com`.

Index

Thank you for buying
3D Printing with SketchUp

About Packt Publishing

Packt, pronounced 'packed', published its first book "*Mastering phpMyAdmin for Effective MySQL Management*" in April 2004 and subsequently continued to specialize in publishing highly focused books on specific technologies and solutions.

Our books and publications share the experiences of your fellow IT professionals in adapting and customizing today's systems, applications, and frameworks. Our solution based books give you the knowledge and power to customize the software and technologies you're using to get the job done. Packt books are more specific and less general than the IT books you have seen in the past. Our unique business model allows us to bring you more focused information, giving you more of what you need to know, and less of what you don't.

Packt is a modern, yet unique publishing company, which focuses on producing quality, cutting-edge books for communities of developers, administrators, and newbies alike. For more information, please visit our website: www.packtpub.com.

About Packt Open Source

In 2010, Packt launched two new brands, Packt Open Source and Packt Enterprise, in order to continue its focus on specialization. This book is part of the Packt Open Source brand, home to books published on software built around Open Source licenses, and offering information to anybody from advanced developers to budding web designers. The Open Source brand also runs Packt's Open Source Royalty Scheme, by which Packt gives a royalty to each Open Source project about whose software a book is sold.

Writing for Packt

We welcome all inquiries from people who are interested in authoring. Book proposals should be sent to author@packtpub.com. If your book idea is still at an early stage and you would like to discuss it first before writing a formal book proposal, contact us; one of our commissioning editors will get in touch with you.

We're not just looking for published authors; if you have strong technical skills but no writing experience, our experienced editors can help you develop a writing career, or simply get some additional reward for your expertise.

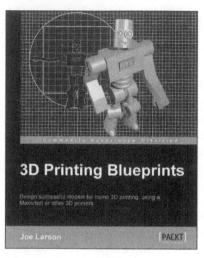

3D Printing Blueprints

ISBN: 978-1-84969-708-8   Paperback: 310 pages

Design successful models for home 3D printing, using a Makerbot or other 3D printers

1. Design 3D models that will print successfully using Blender, a free 3D modeling program.

2. Customize, edit, repair, and then share your creations on Makerbot's Thingiverse website.

3. Easy-to-follow guide on 3D printing; learn to create a new model at the end of each chapter.

Blender 3D Printing Essentials

ISBN: 978-1-78328-459-7   Paperback: 114 pages

Bring your ideas to life in Blender and learn how to design beautiful, light, and strong 3D printed objects

1. Design beautiful, colorful, and practical objects in Blender to print or export.

2. Master Blender's special 3D printing tools to maximize print quality and minimize cost.

3. Consider requirements unique to 3D printing such as structural integrity and stability.

Please check **www.PacktPub.com** for information on our titles